CAPITAL PUNISHMENT UPDATE

CAPITAL PUNISHMENT UPDATE

LORRAINE V. COYNE
EDITOR

Nova Science Publishers, Inc.
New York

For permission to use material from this book please contact us:
Telephone 631-231-7269; Fax 631-231-8175
Web Site: http://www.novapublishers.com

LIBRARY OF CONGRESS CATALOGING-IN-PUBLICATION DATA

Capital punishment update / Lorraine V. Coyne, editor.
p. cm.
ISBN 978-1-60456-133-3 (hardcover)
1. Capital punishment--United States. 2. Capital punishment--United States--Cases. I. Coyne, Lorraine V.
KF9227.C2C37 2007
345.73'0773--dc22 2007044351

Published by Nova Science Publishers, Inc. ✦ New York

Contents

PREFACE

The issue of capital punishment will not go away. This new book presents new and significant analyses related to recent Supreme Court cases and new books on the topic.

Chapter 1 - Most capital offenses are state crimes. In 1994, however, Congress revived the death penalty as a federal sentencing option. More than a few federal statutes now proscribe offenses punishable by death. A number of bills have been offered during the 110th Congress to modify federal law in the area. One, S. 447 (Sen. Feingold), would abolish the federal death penalty. Others would increase the number of capital offenses to include one or more newly created offenses or existing non-capital offenses newly designated as capital offenses, *e.g.*, H.R. 855 (Rep. Lungren), H.R. 880 (Rep. Forbes), H.R. 1118 (Rep. Keller), H.R. 1645 (Rep. Gutierrez), H.R. 2376 (Rep. Franks), H.R. 3147 (Rep. Wilson), H.R. 3150 (Rep. Keller), H.R. 3156 (Rep. Lamar Smith), S. 330 (Sen. Isakson), S. 607 (Sen. Vitter), S. 1320 (Sen. Kyl), S. 1348 (Sen. Reid), and S. 1860 (Sen. Cornyn).

Numbered among the new capital offenses and newly designated capital offenses are murder related to street gang offenses or Travel Act violations, murder committed during and in relation to drug trafficking, murder committed in the course of evading border inspection, murder of disaster assistance workers, and various terrorism-related murders.

A third category of proposals would adjust in one way or another the procedures used to try and sentence capital defendants, including those relating to where a capital offense may be tried, the appointment of counsel in capital cases, the pre-trial notification which the parties must exchange in capital cases, the procedures that apply when the defendant claims to be mentally retarded, adjustments in the statutory aggravating and mitigating circumstances, jury matters, and the site of federal executions. Among the bills offering one or more of these proposals are: H.R. 851 (Rep. Gohmert), H.R. 880 (Rep. Forbes), H.R. 1645 (Rep. Gutierrez), H.R. 1914 (Rep. Carter), H.R. 3150 (Rep. Keller), H.R. 3153 (Rep. Gerlach), H.R. 3156 (Rep. Lamar Smith), S. 1320 (Sen. Kyl), and S. 1860 (Sen. Cornyn).

Chapter 2 - With the passage of P.L. 103-322, the Violent Crime Control and Law Enforcement Act of 1994, the federal death penalty became available as a possible punishment for a substantial number of new and existing civilian offenses. On April 24, 1996, the Antiterrorism and Effective Death Penalty Act of 1996 made further modifications and additions to the list of federal capital crimes. On June 25, 2002, P.L. 107-197, the Terrorist Bombings Convention Implementation Act of 2002, added another capital crime to the United States Code. The Intelligence Reform and Terrorism Prevention Act of 2004, P.L. 108-458, enacted December 17, 2004, included provisions which impacted or expanded some of the existing death penalty provisions. This article lists the current federal capital offenses and summarizes the procedures for federal civilian death penalty cases.

Chapter 3 - During its 2006-2007 term the Supreme Court announced decisions in eight capital cases. Three arose under a later abandoned Texas procedure that restricted jury consideration of mitigation evidence to evidence of intent, future dangerousness and victim provocation. In one, *Smith v. Texas*, the Court held that the defendant's failure to challenging the state's insufficient corrective adjustments in the procedure could not be used to deny him the benefit of a less demanding test to assess the harm caused by use of the challenged, defective underlying procedure. In another, *Abdul-Kabir v. Quarterman*, it rejected the suggestion that the Court's earlier cases permitted the use of the mitigating evidence-restricting procedure as long as the evidence in question related at least in part to one of the narrow factors that the procedure allowed to be considered. In the third, *Brewer v. Quarterman*, it rejected the suggestion that the Court's earlier cases permitted the use of the mitigating evidence-restricting procedure as long as the procedure permitted "sufficient" consideration of the evidence in question given its quality and weight.

Earlier in the term in *Ayers v. Belmontes*, the Court concluded that the feature in California's capital sentencing procedure that permits consideration to any evidence that extenuated the gravity of the crime allowed a jury from giving full effect to mitigating evidence of the defendant's character and background even if otherwise unrelated to the crime.

In *Uttecht v. Brown*, the Court held that appellate courts should give considerable deference to a trial judge's dismissal of a prospective capital juror for cause. In *Schriro v. Landrigan*, it found that the absence of prejudice doomed an ineffectiveness of counsel challenge based on trial counsel's failure to search for mitigating evidence. In *Lawrence v. Florida*, it construed the federal habeas statute of limitations and concluded that the statute was not tolled pending a petition for Supreme Court review of state collateral review decisions (e.g. state habeas corpus decisions). In *Panelli v. Quarterman*, it determined that the limitation on second or successive habeas petitions posed no impediment to consideration of a petition which challenged the execution of a mentally incompetent death row inmate.

Chapter 4 - During the 2005-2006 Term, the Supreme Court gave favorable decisions to the defendants in three out of the six death penalty cases it announced. In *Hill v. McDonough,* the Court ruled unanimously that the method-of-lethal injection claims can be brought under 42 U.S.C. § 1983 rather than under the *habeas corpus* statute (28 U.S.C. §2254). In *House v. Bell*, a case involving a death row inmate who claimed that DNA evidence proved he did not commit the crime for which he was found guilty, the Court found in a 5 -3 ruling that the petitioner had satisfied the "gateway" standard for habeas review, but left open the question of whether the Constitution precludes execution of an "innocent" defendant found guilty and sentenced following a constitutionally adequate trial. In *Holmes v. South Carolina,* the Court unanimously held that a capital defendant cannot be denied the right to introduce evidence of third party guilt. The other cases, in which the Court upheld application of state death penalty statutes, appear to reveal a greater division among the justices over the fairness of capital punishment. The 5-4 decision in *Kansas v. Marsh* centered around a debate concerning capital punishment as much as it did a ruling on the unusual statute in Kansas which provided that juries should sentence a defendant to die – rather than serve life in prison – when the evidence for and against imposing death is equal. In *Brown v. Sanders*, a second 5-4 decision, the Court upheld the petitioner's death sentence even though two of the sentencing factors presented to the jury were declared invalid. In *Oregon v. Guzek*, the Court held that states may reasonably refuse to allow convicted capital defendants to offer alibi evidence for the first time at the sentencing phase of their trials; two Justices would have permitted the exclusion of any evidence at sentencing that cast doubt upon the jury's guilty verdict, but the majority were obviously unwilling to go that far.

In: Capital Punishment Update
Editor: Lorraine V. Coyne, pp. 1-47
ISBN: 978-1-60456-133-3

Chapter 1

THE DEATH PENALTY: CAPITAL PUNISHMENT LEGISLATION IN THE 110TH CONGRESS*

Charles Doyle Senior

ABSTRACT

Most capital offenses are state crimes. In 1994, however, Congress revived the death penalty as a federal sentencing option. More than a few federal statutes now proscribe offenses punishable by death. A number of bills have been offered during the 110th Congress to modify federal law in the area. One, S. 447 (Sen. Feingold), would abolish the federal death penalty. Others would increase the number of capital offenses to include one or more newly created offenses or existing non-capital offenses newly designated as capital offenses, *e.g.*, H.R. 855 (Rep. Lungren), H.R. 880 (Rep. Forbes), H.R. 1118 (Rep. Keller), H.R. 1645 (Rep. Gutierrez), H.R. 2376 (Rep. Franks), H.R. 3147 (Rep. Wilson), H.R. 3150 (Rep. Keller), H.R. 3156 (Rep. Lamar Smith), S. 330 (Sen. Isakson), S. 607 (Sen. Vitter), S. 1320 (Sen. Kyl), S. 1348 (Sen. Reid), and S. 1860 (Sen. Cornyn).

Numbered among the new capital offenses and newly designated capital offenses are murder related to street gang offenses or Travel Act violations, murder committed during and in relation to drug trafficking, murder committed in the course of evading border inspection, murder of disaster assistance workers, and various terrorism-related murders.

A third category of proposals would adjust in one way or another the procedures used to try and sentence capital defendants, including those

---

* Excerpted from CRS Report RL34163, dated September 7, 2007.

relating to where a capital offense may be tried, the appointment of counsel in capital cases, the pre-trial notification which the parties must exchange in capital cases, the procedures that apply when the defendant claims to be mentally retarded, adjustments in the statutory aggravating and mitigating circumstances, jury matters, and the site of federal executions. Among the bills offering one or more of these proposals are: H.R. 851 (Rep. Gohmert), H.R. 880 (Rep. Forbes), H.R. 1645 (Rep. Gutierrez), H.R. 1914 (Rep. Carter), H.R. 3150 (Rep. Keller), H.R. 3153 (Rep. Gerlach), H.R. 3156 (Rep. Lamar Smith), S. 1320 (Sen. Kyl), and S. 1860 (Sen. Cornyn).

INTRODUCTION

Most capital punishment cases are state cases.[1] There are several federal crimes, however, for which the death penalty is a sentencing option.[2] The 110th Congress has seen proposals to abolish the federal death penalty, to increase the number of federal capital offenses, and to adjust the procedure under which capital cases are tried and sentencing determinations are made. This is an overview of some of those proposals.

CURRENT PROCEDURE

Existing federal law treats capital cases differently. There is no statute of limitations for capital offenses.[3] There is a preference for the trial of capital cases in the county in which they occur.[4] Defendants in capital cases are entitled to two attorneys, one of whom "shall be learned in the law applicable to capital cases."[5] The Attorney General must ultimately approve the decision to seek the death penalty in any given case.[6] Defendants are entitled to notice when the prosecution intends to seek the death penalty,[7] and at least three days before the trial, to a copy of the indictment as well as a list of the government's witnesses and names in the jury pool.[8] Defendants have twice as many peremptory jury challenges in capital cases as in other felony cases and prosecutors more than three times as many.[9] Should the defendant be found guilty of a capital offense the sentencing hearing procedures set forth in chapter 228 of title 18 of the United States Code come into play.

The chapter divides federal capital offenses into three categories for purposes of determining whether the death penalty should be imposed in light of the aggravating and mitigating facts presented in the case.[10] The first group consists of espionage and treason;[11] the second, of homicide offenses;[12] and the third, of drug offenses.[13]

In homicide cases, the sentencing hearing involves two determinations: whether the defendant acted with the intent required in section 3591(a)(2) of the chapter and whether the weighing of the pertinent aggravating and mitigating circumstances warrant imposition of the death penalty in section 3592(c). In order to keep the two inquiries distinct and to avoid confusion and unfair prejudice, federal courts will generally permit the inquiries to be conduct sequentially.[14]

The same list of mitigating factors applies to each of the three categories of capital offenses. The list consists of seven specific statutory factors – impaired capacity, minor participation, disparate treatment of codefendants, no prior criminal record, mental or emotional disturbance, and victim consent – but also includes a catch-all, open-ended factor.[15]

Each of the three categories has its own list of statutory aggravating factors. They share a catch-all, open-ended aggravating factor available for each of the three categories of capital offenses which the jury may weigh,[16] but the death penalty may only be imposed after first finding at least one of the more specific, designated aggravating factors.[17]

The list of designated aggravating factors relating to espionage and treason is the shortest of the three: prior espionage or treason conviction, grave risk to national security, and grave risk of death.[18] The list of the designated homicide aggravating factors contains sixteen entries, including the fact that the murder was committed during the course of one of group of other federal offenses.[19] The drug aggravating factors focus on prior convictions, the risk to children, the use of firearms, and lethal adulteration.[20]

The jury must unanimously agree that an aggravating factor has been established before the factor may be weighed in determining whether to impose the death penalty; on the other hand the finding of a single juror is sufficient for consideration of a mitigating factor.[21] The death penalty may only be imposed if the jury unanimously finds that the aggravating factors outweigh the mitigating factors; or if the court so finds in the absence of a jury.[22]

PROCEDURAL CHANGES

During the 110th Congress, proposals have been offered that would modify existing law relating to:

- where a capital offense may be tried, - the appointment of counsel in capital cases,
- the pre-trial notification which the parties must exchange in capital cases, - the procedures that apply when the defendant claims to be mentally retarded, - adjustments in the statutory aggravating and mitigating circumstances, - jury matters, and - the site of federal executions.

Venue and Vicinage

Generally

The Constitution provides that "the trial of all crimes . . . shall be held in the state where the said crimes shall have been committed; but when not committed within any State, the trial shall be at such place or places as the Congress may by law have directed,"[23] and that "in all criminal prosecutions, the accused shall enjoy the right to a speedy and public trial, by an impartial jury of the state and district wherein the crime shall have been committed, which district shall have been previously ascertained by law."[24] From the beginning,[25] Congress has provided in language that now appears in 18 U.S.C. 3235, that where possible capital cases should be tried in the county in which they occur.[26] It has also long specifically provided that murder and manslaughter cases shall be tried where the death-inflicting injury occurs regardless of where the victim dies,[27] as 18 U.S.C. 3236 now states.[28] Furthermore, for some time[29] it has provided in the words of 18 U.S.C. 3237 that multi-district crimes may be tried where they are begun, continued, or completed and that offenses involving the use of the mails, transportation in interstate or foreign commerce, or importation into the United States may be tried in any district from, through, or into which commerce, mail, or imports travel.[30]

Although some of the venue proposals offered in the 110th Congress deal primarily with venue for newly created or newly amended federal capital offenses, H.R. 3156 (Rep. Lamar Smith) and S. 1860 (Sen. Cornyn) address venue in capital cases generally. They strike the language of section 3235 that calls for the trial of capital cases in the county in which they occur if possible. In its place, they install two subsections whose precise scope is somewhat uncertain.[31]

The proposed amendment appears intended to repeal both the "county trial in capital cases" feature of section 3235 and, by indirection, the murder portion of the "murder-manslaughter trial" feature of section 3236.[32] It seems to replicate the continuing offense language of section 3237 with one significant addition; it permits trial where commerce-related conduct occurs. The scope of the proposed amendment is likely to depend in part on the application of constitutional constraints.

The proposed amendment must operate within constitutional venue and vicinage limitations, that is that: "The trial of all crimes . . . shall be held in the state where the said crimes shall have been committed," and that "In all criminal prosecutions, the accused shall enjoy the right to a speedy and public trial, by an impartial jury of the state and district wherein the crime shall have been committed."[33]

The Supreme Court in *United States v. Cabrales* held that in light of these provisions the crime of money laundering committed in Florida could not be tried in Missouri where the laundered funds had been criminally generated – absent other circumstances.[34] Shortly thereafter, the Court held in *United States v. Rodriguez-Moreno*, that the crime of using a firearm during and in relation to the crime of kidnaping could be tried in New Jersey into which the victim had been carried, notwithstanding the fact that the firearm was acquired and used in Maryland after the victim had been moved there from New Jersey.

Cabrales is not as restrictive as it might seem at first; nor is *Rodriguez-Moreno* as permissive. Cabrales laundered the Missouri drug money in Florida, but there was no evidence that she was a member of the Missouri drug trafficking conspiracy or that she had transported the money from Missouri to Florida. The Court acknowledged that she might have been tried in Missouri had either been the case.[35]

Rodriguez-Moreno and his confederates kidnapped a drug trafficking associate and transported him over the course of time from Texas to New Jersey and then to Maryland. Rodriguez-Moreno acquired the firearm with which he threatened the kidnap victim in Maryland but was tried in New Jersey for using a firearm "during and in relation to a crime of violence [kidnaping]" in violation of 18 U.S.C. 924(c)(1). Section 924(c)(1) in the eyes of the Court has "two distinct *conduct elements* . . . using and carrying of a gun and the commission of a kidnaping."[36] A crime with distinct conduct elements may be tried wherever any of those elements occurred; kidnaping is a continuous offense that in this case began in Texas and continued through New Jersey to Maryland; venue over the kidnaping, a conduct element of the section 924(c)(1), was proper in Texas, New Jersey or Maryland; consequently venue over the violation of section 924(c)(1) was proper in either Texas, New Jersey or Maryland.[37]

The Court was quick to distinguish *Cabrales* from *Rodriguez-Moreno*: "The existence of criminally generated proceeds [in *Cabrales*] was a circumstance element of the offense but the proscribed conduct – defendant's money laundering activity –occurred after the fact of the offense begun and completed by others." In

Rodriguez-Moreno, "given the 'during and in relation to' language, the underlying crime of violence is a critical part of the §924(c)(1) offense."[38] Subsequent lower federal appellate courts have read *Cabrales* and *Rodriguez-Moreno* to require that a crime be tried where at least one of its elements occurs.[39]

It is not clear how the proposed venue amendment would fare in light of *Cabrales* and *Rodriguez-Moreno*. It states that "(a) The trial for any offense punishable by death shall be held in the district where the offense was committed or in any district in which the offense began, continued, or was completed. (b) If the offense, or related conduct, under subsection (a) involves activities which affect interstate or foreign commerce, or the importation of an object or person into the United States, such offense may be prosecuted in any district in which those activities occurred."[40] The amendment appears to permit trial of an offense in a district in which related conduct affecting interstate or foreign commerce occurs even if the offense itself and each of its elements is committed entirely in another district.

The *Cabrales*' money generating drug trafficking in Missouri would seem to qualify as "conduct related" to the laundering in Florida for purposes of the proposal, and yet in *Cabrales* that was not enough. Nor would the proposal always appear to meet *Rodriguez-Moreno*'s "conduct element" standard. There is nothing in the proposal that requires that the "related conduct affecting interstate commerce" be an element of the offense to be tried. In fact, the alternative wording – "if the offense, or related conduct . . . involves activities which affect interstate commerce" – seems to contemplate situations in which affecting commerce is not an element, conduct or otherwise, of the offense. Such applications may appear to a reviewing court to be more than the Constitution permits.

Specific Offenses

In the case of proposed venue provisions for new or existing federal capital offenses, one common proposal builds upon the scheme approved in *Rodriguez-Moreno*. The statute before the Court there, 18 U.S.C. 924(c)(1), outlaws the use of a firearm "during and in relation" to a crime of violence or serious drug offense. Several bills – *e.g.*, H.R. 880 (Rep. Forbes), H.R. 3150 (Rep. Keller), H.R. 3156 (Rep. Lamar Smith), and S. 1860 (Sen. Cornyn) – would create a new federal crime, one that prohibits the commission of a crime of violence "during and in relation" to a drug trafficking offense, proposed 21 U.S.C. 865. They permit prosecution for such an offense "in (1) the judicial district in which the murder or other crime of violence occurred; or (2) any judicial district in which the drug trafficking crime may be prosecuted," proposed 21 U.S.C. 865(b).

This analogy to *Rodriguez-Moreno* seems likely to work. The new crime, like section 924(c) in *Rodriguez-Moreno*, has two elements, a crime of violence and a simultaneous, related drug trafficking offense. *Rodriguez-Moreno* involved a continuing offense. Many drug trafficking offenses are likely to be considered continuing offenses for venue purposes,[41] but some may not be. It should not matter. *Rodriguez-Moreno* insists only that the crime may be tried where one of its conduct elements (crime of violence or drug trafficking crime) occur.

The several of the same bills – *e.g.*, H.R. 880 (Rep. Forbes), H.R. 3150 (Rep. Keller), H.R. 3156 (Rep. Lamar Smith), and S. 1860 (Sen. Cornyn) – would add, to the existing federal capital offense of committing a crime of violence in aid of a racketeering (RICO) offense, an explicit venue provision.[42] The addition states that prosecution for a violation of section 1959 may be brought where the crime of violence occurs or where the racketeering activity of the enterprise occurs.[43] Even without the explicit addition, the Second Circuit has held that since a RICO violation is an element of a section 1959 offense, venue for trial of a violation of section 1959 is proper wherever the underlying RICO might be tried, i.e., wherever an element of a RICO violation occurs.[44]

Appointment of Counsel

Capital defendants are entitled to the assignment of two attorneys for their defense.[45] There is some uncertainty over whether they are to be appointed immediately following indictment for a capital offense or whether they need only be appointed "promptly" sometime prior to trial;[46] and whether the right expires with the decision of the government not to seek the death penalty.[47]

The Justice Department expressed concern that under existing law the Fourth Circuit has held that the right to appoint counsel does not expire with the government's decision not to seek the death penalty. The Department also noted the inefficiencies experienced in other circuits in cases where it is clear the death penalty will not be sought but where a second attorney must be retained until the formal decision is announced.[48]

H.R. 851(Rep. Gohmert) would amend section 3005 so that prosecutor's notice of an intent to seek the death penalty, rather than indictment for a capital offense, triggers the right to the appointment of second counsel.[49] Critics have suggested that both the interests of the defendant and the interests of the government are best served by early appointment of counsel, expert in defense of capital cases.[50]

Pre-Trial Notice of Intent to Seek the Death Penalty

Section 3593 obligates the prosecutor to advise the defendant and the court, "a reasonable time before trial" or before the acceptance of a plea, of the government's intention to seek the death penalty.[51] The Fourth and Eleventh Circuits have held that a failure to provide timely notice may preclude the effort of a prosecutor to seek the death penalty. More exactly, they have held (1) that a death notice filed unreasonably close to the date set for trial is properly subject to a motion to strike the government's death notice, without which the government may not seek the death penalty, and (2) that an interlocutory appeal may be taken from the denial of such a motion.[52] The Second Circuit, on the other hand, concluded that section 3593(a) does not create a right to avoid the death penalty because of the government's untimely death notice and that consequently a refusal to strike the death notice is not a matter from which an interlocutory appeal may be taken.[53]

Prosecutors will sometimes provide a "protective death notice" in order to preserve the option to seek the death penalty before a final decision is made. The notice is withdrawn should the Attorney General decide not to seek the death penalty. The arrangement is not one which the Justice Department prefers.[54] On the other hand, both the right to a speedy trial and the fact that the defendant in a capital case is not likely to be free on bail prior to trial may argue for such incentives for expeditious prosecutorial determinations.

H.R. 851 (Rep. Gohmert), H.R. 3156 (Rep. Lamar Smith), and S. 1860 (Sen. Cornyn) amend section 3593(a) to authorize a continuance in the face of a delayed notification of an intent to seek the death penalty. They also make it clear that a defendant may not foreclose the government's option by pleading guilty before prosecutors have had time to seek the Attorney General's approval to seek the death penalty.[55]

Pre-Trial Notice of Mitigating Factors

H.R. 851 (Rep. Gohmert), H.R. 3156 (Rep. Lamar Smith), and S. 1860 (Sen. Cornyn) also balance the prosecution's obligation to disclose any aggravating factors upon which it intends to rely with a similar defense obligation to notify the prosecution of mitigating factors upon which it intends to rely when the prosecution seeks the death penalty.[56] Elsewhere once the government has announced its intention to seek the death penalty, the bills afford defendants the advantage of a continuance when necessary to address the additional issues raised.[57] Here, it affords the prosecution a similar benefit.[58] Critics may question the symmetry.[59]

Mental Retardation

Neither the insanity defense nor the prohibitions against trial of the mentally incompetent necessarily preclude prosecution and conviction of the mentally retarded.[60] Nevertheless, section 3592(a) seems to permit evidence of mental retardation as a mitigating factor under section 3592(a)(1) (impaired capacity), 3592(a)(6)(disturbance), or 3592(a)(8)(mitigation generally).[61] Moreover, neither the Constitution nor federal statutory provisions allow the execution of a federal capital defendant suffering from mental retardation.[62]

The limited available case law suggests – with some exception – that the determination of the issue may be assigned to the court (rather than the jury) to be established by the defendant under preponderance of the evidence standard prior to trial.[63] As for the definition of mental retardation, the Court in *Atkins* cites two clinical definitions of mental retardation,[64] which it encapsulates with the observation that, "As discussed above, clinical definitions of mental retardation require not only subaverage intellectual functioning, but also significant limitations in adaptive skills such as communication, self-care, and self-direction that became manifest before age 18," 536 U.S. at 318.

H.R. 851 (Rep. Gohmert), H.R. 3156 (Rep. Lamar Smith), and S. 1860 (Sen. Cornyn) would make several procedural adjustments to accommodate claims of mental retardation in federal capital cases. First, as noted earlier they establish a reciprocal pre-trial notification requirement. After the prosecution notifies the defendant of its intention to seek the death penalty and of the aggravating factors upon which it intends to rely, the defendant must notify the government of the mitigating factors, including mental retardation, upon which he intends to rely.[65] Second, they call for comparable notice when the defendant intends to claim mental retardation as a bar to execution.[66] Third, they afford the prosecution the right to an independent mental health examination of any defendant claiming retardation and to a continuance to prepare for trial and sentencing if necessary.[67] Fourth, they condition the defendant's presentation of evidence and argument relating to mental retardation, at least for mitigation purposes, to instances where the defendant has provided the required prior notification.[68] Fifth, they state that the defendant bears the burden of establishing mental retardation by a preponderance of the evidence.[69] Sixth, they instruct the trier of fact, be it judge or jury, to consider the issue of mental retardation only if an aggravating factor has been found and if so to consider the issue of mental retardation first among the mitigating factors.[70] Seventh, they provide that a capital defendant found to be mental retarded is be sentenced to imprisonment for a term of years or to life imprisonment without the possibility of release.[71] Eighth, they supply a statutory definition of mental retardation with three components: that the defendant have an IQ of 70 or less, that he have had continuously since under 18 years of age, and that it has continuously impaired mental functions including the ability to learn, reason, and control impulses.[72] The Justice Department endorsed similar legislative proposals in the 109th Congress as a means of introducing consistency into federal practice in the area.[73]

There may be objections, however. The definition of mental retardation might be thought too narrow to embrace all those constitutionally protected.[74] Resolution of mental retardation issues, some would contend, should occur prior to trial as a matter of fairness and judicial economy if nothing else[75] The proposal may also be criticized for its failure to mirror the procedure governing the prosecution's right to an independent mental health examination in the case of insanity defense claims.[76]

Aggravating and Mitigating Factors

Furman v. Georgia, 408 U.S. 238 (1972), condemn state capital punishment procedures, and by implication federal procedures, for failure to reserve the death penalty to the most egregious capital cases. The procedures have been adjusted to provide juries with aggravating and mitigating factors to guide the exercise of their discretion and ensure that the death penalty is only imposed in the most serious cases.

Unequal Codefendant Treatment

Several bills suggest adjustments in the designated aggravating and mitigating circumstances described in section 3592. For instance, some proposals amend the mitigating circumstance that now applies when "another defendant or defendants, equally culpable in the crime, will not be punished by death," H.R. 851 (Rep. Gohmert), H.R. 1914 (Rep. Carter).[77] The amendment limits the factor to instances where the prosecution has elected not to seek the death penalty for a codefendant. In doing so it eliminates from coverage of instances where the defendant's codefendant is under 18 years of age, or mentally retarded, or extradited with an agreement not to execute, or where an earlier jury has declined to sentence a codefendant to death for the same offense.

The amendment might be thought to have largely symbolic impact. Section 3592(a)(8) allows a defendant to offer evidence of "any circumstance of the offense that mitigate[s] against imposition of the death penalty." Thus, it seems that any circumstances removed from a specific statutory mitigating factor might be claimed under the catch-all provisions of section 3592(a)(8). Some commentators have suggested, however, the courts might construe removal as a limitation on the catchall provision as well.[78]

Substantial Planning

Another proposal adds an aggravating factor to the espionage and treason category to cover offenses involving substantial planning, H.R. 1914 (Rep. Carter).[79] Espionage and treason, by their nature, would involve substantial planning in most instances. The proposal would permit imposition of the death penalty even in the absence of any of the other aggravating factors: prior espionage or treason conviction, grave risk to national security, grave risk of death. Treason has been a capital crime almost since the founding of the Republic,[80] but it is not clear that the death penalty may be imposed for any crime that does not involve the taking of a human life.[81] The Constitution may limit the circumstances under which the death penalty may be imposed upon a first time offender, convicted of espionage in a case where there is neither a grave risk to national security nor a grave risk of death.

Murder Plus Felonies

Most federal capital punishment statutes do not proscribe murder as such. They outlaw murder under particular circumstances, circumstances that themselves might be considered aggravating, such as the murder of a Member of Congress or a murder committed in conjunction with the rape of the victim. Section 3592(c)(1) recognizes as an aggravating factor that murder was during the course of one of a list of designated federal crimes.

Several bills place other offenses on the list. H.R. 851 (Rep. Gohmert) would add receipt of military training from a foreign terrorist organization (18 U.S.C. 2332D) to section 3592(c)(1).[82] H.R. 851 and other bills would insert additional offenses including:

- 18 U.S.C. 241 (conspiracy against civil rights),
- 18 U.S.C. 245 (federal protected rights),
- 18 U.S.C. 247 (interference with religious exercise),

- 18 U.S.C. 37 (violence at international airports),
- 18 U.S.C. 1512 (witness tampering), and
- 18 U.S.C. 1513 (retaliating against a witness), H.R. 851 (Rep. Gohmert), H.R. 3156 (Rep. Lamar Smith), S. 1860 (S. Cronyn).[83]

The rationale for expansion appears to be that (1) capital punishment should be reserved for the "worst of the worst;" (2) murders committed in the course of the most serious federal crimes fit that description; and (3) one or more such most serious federal crimes are not now listed in section 3592(c)(1).[84] The rationale of opponents seems to be two-fold. First, as with mitigating circumstances, specific designation is less significant when the catch-all provision would allow presentation to the jury in any event. In the case of aggravating circumstances, however, expressly adding new crimes to the "murder plus" factor status is significant because the existence of a specifically designated aggravating factor is a sine qua non for imposition of the penalty; the mere presence of a catch-all aggravating factor is insufficient. Second, the list of death-qualifying, specifically designated aggravating factors is now so close to all-encompassing that some special justification may be in order before the list is expanded.[85]

Obstruction of Justice

The creation of a new obstruction of justice aggravating factor is a common proposal, H.R. 851 (Rep. Gohmert); H.R. 1914 (Rep. Carter), H.R. 3156 (Rep. Lamar Smith), S. 1860 (Sen. Cornyn).[86] The proposal rests on the premise that killing witnesses and other participants in the judicial process "strikes at the heart of the system of justice itself."[87] Critics suggest that its breadth threatens to push the federal system to a point where it has made all murders capital, where the exceptions to the "narrowing" use of aggravating factors have eliminated any narrowing impact.[88]

Previous Firearm Conviction

Section 3592(c)(2) now recognizes as a statutory aggravating factor the fact that:

> *For any offense, other than an offense for which a sentence of death is sought on the basis of section 924(c),* the defendant has previously been convicted of a Federal or State offense punishable by a term of imprisonment of more than 1 year, involving the use or attempted or threatened use of a firearm (as defined in section 921) against another person. [Emphasis added.]

Section 924(c) provides additional penalties when a defendant uses or possesses a firearm during and in relation to the commission of a federal crime of violence or drug trafficking. Violation is a capital offense when in the course of the crime the firearm is used to commit a murder.[89] The italicized portion of section 3593(c)(2) is open to interpretation,[90] and several proposals strike the language. H.R. 851 (Rep.Gohmert), H.R. 3156 (Rep. Lamar Smith), S. 1860 (Sen. Cornyn). One of the bills, H.R. 851 (Rep. Gohmert), amends section 3592(c)(2) further to make it clear that the new provision does not cover the conviction that has resulted in the capital sentencing hearing at issue, but only prior adjudications resulting in firearms conviction.[91]

One critic has argued that in view of the breadth of section 924(c) the amendment would make an aggravating factor out of the possession of a firearm during any federal crime of violence or drug trafficking that ended in murder.[92]

Pecuniary Gain

Section 3592(c)(8) is what might be taken for a murder-for-hire aggravating factor: "The defendant committed the offense as consideration for the receipt, or in expectation of the receipt of anything of pecuniary value." A casual reading might suggest that the factor covers murder for hire when the murder is paid either before or after the murder. Instead, the courts have concluded that the phrase "as consideration for" covers the for-hire murders, and the phrase "in expectation of the receipt" covers murders from which there is a more general anticipated gain.[93]

Yet the factor only applies when the murder was motivated by monetary gain. It is not enough that the gain was incidental to or a consequence of the murder.[94]

The Justice Department has suggested that as now worded the factor is susceptible to uneven application since it does not include instances where the murder is committed to preserve a defendant's ill-gotten treasure.[95] There are proposed amendments that address the issue by altering the section to read: The defendant committed the offense as consideration for the receipt, or in expectation of the receipt, *or in order to retain illegal possession* of anything of pecuniary value, H.R. 851 (Rep. Gohmert), H.R. 3156 (Rep. Lamar Smith), S. 1860 (Sen. Cornyn).

The amendment would like bring most murders committed incidental to a robbery within the factor's purview. The objections voiced over other aggravating factor amendments may be heard again: "Run of the mill" murders are being made capital. The death penalty is no longer reserved for the worst of the worst murderers. This is the situation the Court found unacceptable in *Furman*. Or so the argument may run.

Murder of a Law Enforcement Officer

H.R. 3153 (Rep. Gerlach) would make an aggravating factor of the fact that the murder victim was a law enforcement officer.[96] Murder of a federal law enforcement officer during or on account of the performance of his or her duties is already an aggravating factor.[97] The amendment would expand the factor to include state law enforcement officers, federal law enforcement officer murdered other than during or on account of the performance of their official duties, and attempts to kill either state or federal law enforcement officers.

Sympathy, Prejudice and other Arbitrary Factors

In *California v. Brown*, the Supreme Court upheld a state court instruction which informed a capital jury that "they must not be swayed by mere sentiment, conjecture, sympathy, passion, prejudice, public opinion or public feeling."[98] H.R. 851 (Rep. Gohmert) introduces a similar directive into the federal process in capital cases.[99] H.R. 3156 (Rep. Lamar Smith) and S. 1860 (Sen. Cornyn) would use the same language but drop references to "sentiment" and "sympathy,"[100] perhaps in response to criticism of an earlier version of the proposal.[101]

Elimination of the Term-of-Years Option

Many federal capital punishment statutes offer but two sentencing alternatives, death or life imprisonment.[102] Several others, however, offer a third option: imprisonment for any term of years.[103] In recognition of this fact, existing law states that if no aggravating factors are found to exist "the court shall impose a sentence other than death authorized by law."[104] And if the trier of fact finds that the death penalty should not be imposed in spite of the presence of one or more aggravating factors, existing law calls for "life imprisonment without possibility of release or *some other lesser sentence*."[105] Several proposals, H.R. 3156 (Rep. Lamar Smith), S. 1860 (Sen. Cornyn), and H.R. 851 (Rep. Gohmert) among them, would eliminate the possibility of a sentence for a term of years, if one of the aggravating factors is found.[106]

Capital Juries

A number of proposals in the 110th Congress address problems associated with selecting and maintaining a panel of qualified jurors in capital cases. Existing law states the jury at the sentencing phase of a capital case "shall consist of 12 members, unless, at any time before the conclusion of the hearing, the parties stipulate with the approval of the court, that it shall consist of a lesser number."[107] H.R.851 (Rep. Gohmert) and H.R. 1914 (Rep. Carter) would amend the provision to permit the court to approve a lesser number for good cause, without requiring the approval of the defendant or the prosecutor.[108] Imposition of the death penalty upon the recommendation of a jury of less than twelve members over the objection of the defendant is likely to draw criticism.[109] Perhaps to ensure that recourse to juries of less than twelve will only be necessary in extreme cases, the two bills increase the number of permissible alternate jurors from six to nine and afford each side four addition peremptory challenges in the cases where more than six alternates are impaneled.[110] H.R. 851 (Gohmert) also amends section 3592 to discourage the dismissal of alternate jurors in capital cases until sentencing has been completed.[111] Other proposals, notably H.R. 3156 (Rep. Lamar Smith) and S. 1860 (Sen. Cornyn), leave the number of jurors and alternates as is and merely direct the court to retain alternates until sentencing has been completed.[112]

Existing law permits a capital jury to unanimously recommend a sentence of death or life imprisonment without the possibility of release;[113] if they do not, the court is to sentence the defendant to any lesser sentence authorized by law, *i.e.*, imprisonment for life or for a term of years.[114] H.R. 1914 (Rep. Carter) provides that if the jury cannot agree on a capital recommendation, a new sentencing hearing must be impaneled and new sentencing hearing conducted.[115]

Site of Execution

Existing law provides that the states are to execute federal death sentences.[116] H.R. 851 (Rep. Gohmert), H.R. 3156 (Rep. Lamar Smith), and S. 1860 (Sen. Cornyn) would authorize execution in federal facilities as well, pursuant to regulations promulgated by the Attorney General.[117] The change reflects the availability of federal facilities.[118] They also add a confidentiality clause under which the identity of executors and witnesses at the execution may not be publicly disclosed without their consent.[119]

NEW FEDERAL CAPITAL OFFENSES

S. 607 (Sen. Vitter) would outlaw interference with federal disaster relief efforts; when death results from a violation of the proscription, the defendant may be sentenced to death or life imprisonment.[120]

The bills drafted to counter gang violence – *e.g.*, H.R. 3150 (Rep. Keller), H.R. 880 (Rep. Forbes) – frequently include two new federal death penalty offenses. One proscribes the use of interstate facilities with the intent to commit multiple murders and is a capital offense where death results.[121] The second, modeled after the provision that condemned the use of a firearm during or in relation to a crime of violence or a drug offense, outlaws crimes of violence committed during or in relation to a drug trafficking offense and would have made the offense punishable by death if a death results.[122] The murder committed during and in relation to a drug trafficking offense appears as a capital offense in other bills as well (H.R. 1118 (Rep. Keller); H.R. 3156 (Rep. Lamar Smith); S. 1860 (Sen. Cornyn)); as does the new capital multiple murder proposal (H.R. 3156 (Rep. Lamar Smith); S. 1860 (Sen. Cornyn)). In addition, H.R. 3150 condemns murder along with other violent crimes in furtherance or in aid of a criminal street gang, an offense it makes punishable by death.[123]

Existing law proscribes overseas murder and assault committed against Americans by terrorists, 18 U.S.C. 2332. H.R. 2376 (Rep. Franks), H.R. 3147 (Rep. Wilson), H.R. 3156 (Rep. Lamar Smith), S. 1320 (Sen. Kyl), and S. 1860 (Sen. Cornyn) would proscribe overseas kidnaping of Americans by terrorists and propose the death penalty as a sentencing option when a death results.

Several of the immigration bills – *e.g.*, H.R. 1645 (Rep. Gutierrez), S. 330 (Sen. Isakson), S. 1348 (Sen. Reid) – would proscribe evasion of border inspection and make the offenses punishable by death, imprisonment for any term of years, or for life if death results from a violation, proposed 18 U.S.C. 556.

Rather than amend existing non-capital federal terrorist offenses to make them capital offenses when they result in a death, H.R. 855 (Rep. Lungren), H.R. 3156 (Rep. Lamar Smith), and S. 1860 (Sen. Cornyn) would create a new separate federal offense which outlaws the commission of, or attempt or conspiracy to commit various federal terrorist offenses when a death results, proposed 18 U.S.C. 2339E. Violations are punishable by death or imprisonment for any term of years or for life.[124] Its impact is less dramatic than might appear at first glance since many of its predicate offenses are already capital crimes or are elevated to capital offenses elsewhere in the bills. Nevertheless, as a consequence of section 2339E the following would become capital offenses when a death occurs during the course of their commission:

- 18 U.S.C. 81 (arson within special maritime and territorial jurisdiction), - 18 U.S.C. 175 or 175b (biological weapons),
- 18 U.S.C. 351 (congressional, cabinet, and Supreme Court murder or kidnaping),
- 18 U.S.C. 831 (nuclear materials),
- 18 U.S.C. 842(m) or (n) (plastic explosives),
- 18 U.S.C. 956(a)(1) (conspiracy to murder, kidnap, or maim persons abroad),
- 18 U.S.C. 1030(a)(1), 1030(a)(5)(A)(i)(protection of computers),
- 18 U.S.C. 1361 (destruction of government property or contracts),
- 18 U.S.C. 1362 (destruction of communication lines, stations, or systems),
- 18 U.S.C. 1366(a) (destruction of an energy facility),
- 18 U.S.C. 2155 (destruction of national defense materials, premises, or utilities),
- 18 U.S.C. 2156 (national defense material, premises, or utilities),
- 18 U.S.C. 2332d (financial transactions with terrorist supporting countries),
- 18 U.S.C. 2339 (harboring terrorists),
- 18 U.S.C. 2339A (providing material support to terrorists),[125]
- 18 U.S.C. 2339B (providing material support to terrorist organizations),
- 18 U.S.C. 2339C (financing of terrorism),
- 18 U.S.C. 2339D (military-type training from a foreign terrorist organization),
- 18 U.S.C. 2340A (torture),
- 21 U.S.C. 960a (narco-terrorism),
- 42 U.S.C. 2122 (prohibitions governing atomic weapons),
- 42 U.S.C. 2284 (sabotage of nuclear facilities or fuel),
- 49 U.S.C. 46504 (second sentence)(assault on a flight crew with a dangerous weapon),
- 49 U.S.C. 46505(b)(3) or (c) (explosive or incendiary devices, or endangerment of human life by means of weapons, on aircraft),
- 49 U.S.C. 60123(b) (destruction of interstate gas or hazardous liquid pipeline facility).

On the other hand, some of predicate offenses do not outlaw attempts to violate their proscriptions. In these cases section 2339E establishes not only a new federal capital offense but a new federal crime when death results from the attempt:

- 18 U.S.C. 1203 (hostage taking), - 18 U.S.C. 2339 (harboring terrorists),
- 18 U.S.C. 2339D (receipt of foreign terrorist military training).

CAPITAL PUNISHMENT FOR EXISTING NON-CAPITAL OFFENSES

H.R. 855 (Rep. Lungren), H.R. 3156 (Rep. Lamar Smith), H.R. 3147 (Rep. Wilson), and S. 1860 (Sen. Cornyn) would establish the death penalty as a sentencing option when death results as a consequence of a violation of: 18 U.S.C. 832 (participation in foreign programs involving weapons of mass destruction); 18 U.S.C. 2332g (anti-aircraft missile offenses); 42 U.S.C. 2272 (atomic weapons offenses); 18 U.S.C. 2332h (radiological dispersal device offenses); and 18 U.S.C. 175c (variola virus (small pox) offenses).

The gang bills rewrite the federal criminal gang statute (18 U.S.C. 521) to permit imposition of capital punishment for a death-resulting violation of the newly crafted provisions whose predicate offenses include various crimes of violence, money laundering, drug offenses, credit card fraud, Travel Act violations, and interstate transportation of stolen property, H.R. 880 (Rep. Forbes), H.R. 3150 (Rep. Keller). H.R. 3156 (Rep. Lamar Smith) and S. 1860 (Sen. Cornyn) have the same proposal.

The Travel Act, 18 U.S.C. 1952, among other things, outlaws interstate travel to commit a crime of violence in furtherance of various drug, gambling, or extortion offenses. H.R. 3156 (Rep. Lamar Smith) and S. 1850 (Sen. Cornyn) permit imposition of the death penalty when a violation results in death.[126]

ABOLITION OF CAPITAL PUNISHMENT

S. 447 (Sen. Feingold) eliminates the death penalty as a sentencing option for federal and military capital offenses. It prohibits imposition of the death penalty and provides that prisoners under sentence of death at the time of enactment shall be sentenced to life imprisonment without the possibility of release. It repeals the procedures for implementation of the death penalty, 18 U.S.C. ch. 228. It strikes as well 18 U.S.C. 3235 which dictates that the trial of a capital offense be conducted in the county in which it occurred. It amends the statute of limitations of 18 U.S.C. 3281 to list specific previous capital offenses which may be tried at any time. It makes comparable adjustments in the Code of Military Justice.

Statute of Limitations

The general statute of limitations for federal crimes is 5 years, 18 U.S.C. 3282. Federal crimes punishable by death may be prosecuted at any time, 18 U.S.C. 3281. Federal crimes of terrorism as defined in 18 U.S.C. 2332b(g)(5)(B) that result in death or involve a risk of death may also be prosecuted at any time, 18 U.S.C. 3286(b). Moreover, federal sexual offenses and crimes against children proscribed by 18 U.S.C. 1201 or 18 U.S.C. chs. 109A (sexual abuse), 110 (sexual exploitation f children), or 117(travel of illicit sexual purposes) may likewise be brought any time, 18 U.S.C. 3299.

S. 447 would replaces the language of section 3281 for crimes carrying the death penalty with a list of federal crimes (now punishable by death) which may be prosecuted at any time notwithstanding the bill's elimination of the death penalty.[127] The list is not exhaustive. Some of the omissions are covered by exceptions for crimes against children, sex offenses, or the federal crimes of terrorism. Some are not. The crimes which now can be prosecuted at any time but which S. 447 appears to make subject to the general 5-year statute of limitations are violations of:

- *7 U.S.C. 2146* (killing federal animal transportation inspectors)
- *15 U.S.C. 1825(a)(2)(C)* (killing those enforcing the Horse Protection Act)
- *18 U.S.C. 115(a)(1)(A)* (murder of a family member of a United States officer, employee or judge with intent to impede or retaliate for performance of federal duties)
- *18 U.S.C. 115(a)(1)(B)* (murder of a former United States officer, employee or judge or any member of their families in retaliation for performance of federal duties)
- *18 U.S.C. 229* (death resulting from chemical weapons)
- *18 U.S.C.1119* (murder of a U.S. national by another outside the U.S.)
- *18 U.S.C.1120* (murder by a person who has previously escaped from a federal prison)
- *18 U.S.C.1201* (kidnaping where death of an adult results)
- *18 U.S.C.1503* (murder to obstruct federal judicial proceedings)
- *18 U.S.C. 1513* (retaliatory murder of a federal witness or informant)
- *18 U.S.C. 3261*(murder committed by members of the United States armed forces or accompanying or employed by the United States armed forces overseas)

- *21 U.S.C.461(c)* (murder of federal poultry inspectors during or because of official duties)
- *21 U.S.C.675* (murder of federal meat inspectors during or because of official duties)
- *21 U.S.C. 848(c), 18 U.S.C. 3592b)*(major drug kingpins and attempted murder by drug kingpins to obstruct justice)
- *21 U.S.C.1041(c)* (murder of an egg inspector during or because of official duties)
- *42 U.S.C.2283* (murder of federal nuclear inspectors during or because of official duties).

APPENDIX

Federal Rules of Criminal Procedure: Rule 12.2

(a) Notice of an Insanity Defense. A defendant who intends to assert a defense of insanity at the time of the alleged offense must so notify an attorney for the government in writing within the time provided for filing a pretrial motion, or at any later time the court sets, and file a copy of the notice with the clerk. A defendant who fails to do so cannot rely on an insanity defense. The court may, for good cause, allow the defendant to file the notice late, grant additional trial-preparation time, or make other appropriate orders.

(b) Notice of Expert Evidence of a Mental Condition. If a defendant intends to introduce expert evidence relating to a mental disease or defect or any other mental condition of the defendant bearing on either (1) the issue of guilt or (2) the issue of punishment in a capital case, the defendant must--within the time provided for filing a pretrial motion or at any later time the court sets--notify an attorney for the government in writing of this intention and file a copy of the notice with the clerk. The court may, for good cause, allow the defendant to file the notice late, grant the parties additional trial-preparation time, or make other appropriate orders.

(c) Mental Examination.

(1) Authority to Order an Examination; Procedures.

(A) The court may order the defendant to submit to a competency examination under 18 U.S.C. § 4241.

(B) If the defendant provides notice under Rule 12.2(a), the court must, upon the government's motion, order the defendant to be examined under 18 U.S.C. § 4242. If the defendant provides notice under Rule 12.2(b) the court may, upon the government's motion, order the defendant to be examined under procedures ordered by the court.

(2) Disclosing Results and Reports of Capital Sentencing Examination. The results and reports of any examination conducted solely under Rule 12.2(c)(1) after notice under Rule 12.2(b)(2) must be sealed and must not be disclosed to any attorney for the government or the defendant unless the defendant is found guilty of one or more capital crimes and the defendant confirms an intent to offer during sentencing proceedings expert evidence on mental condition.

(3) Disclosing Results and Reports of the Defendant's Expert Examination. After disclosure under Rule 12.2(c)(2) of the results and reports of the government's examination, the defendant must disclose to the government the results and reports of any examination on mental condition conducted by the defendant's expert about which the defendant intends to introduce expert evidence.

(4) Inadmissibility of a Defendant's Statements. No statement made by a defendant in the course of any examination conducted under this rule (whether conducted with or without the defendant's consent), no testimony by the expert based on the statement, and no other fruits of the statement may be admitted into evidence against the defendant in any criminal proceeding except on an issue regarding mental condition on which the defendant: (A) has introduced evidence of incompetency or evidence requiring notice under Rule 12.2(a) or (b)(1), or (B) has introduced expert evidence in a capital sentencing proceeding requiring notice under Rule 12.2(b)(2).

(d) Failure to Comply.

(1) *Failure to Give Notice or to Submit to Examination.* The court may exclude any expert evidence from the defendant on the issue of the defendant's mental disease, mental defect, or any other mental condition bearing on the defendant's guilt or the issue of punishment in a capital case if the defendant fails to: (A) give notice under Rule 12.2(b); or (B) submit to an examination when ordered under Rule 12.2(c).

(2) *Failure to Disclose.* The court may exclude any expert evidence for which the defendant has failed to comply with the disclosure requirement of Rule 12.2(c)(3).

(e) Inadmissibility of Withdrawn Intention. Evidence of an intention as to which notice was given under Rule 12.2(a) or (b), later withdrawn, is not, in any civil or criminal proceeding, admissible against the person who gave notice of the intention.

Federal Crimes Punishable by Death

- *7 U.S.C. 2146* (murder of a federal animal transportation inspector) *8 U.S.C. 1324* (death resulting from smuggling aliens into the U.S.) *15 U.S.C. 1825(a)(2)(C)* (killing those enforcing the Horse Protection Act) *18 U.S.C. 32* (death resulting from destruction of aircraft or their facilities)
- *18 U.S.C. 33* (death resulting from destruction of motor vehicles or their facilities used in United States foreign commerce)
- *18 U.S.C. 36* (murder by drive-by shooting)
- *18 U.S.C. 37* (death resulting from violence at international airports)
- *18 U.S.C. 115(a)(1)(A)* (murder of a family member of a United States officer, employee or judge with intent to impede or retaliate for performance of federal duties)
- *18 U.S.C. 115(a)(1)(B)* (murder of a former United States officer, employee or judge or any member of their families in retaliation for performance of federal duties)
- *18 U.S.C. 229* (death resulting from chemical weapons offenses)
- *18 U.S.C. 241* (death resulting from conspiracy against civil rights)
- *18 U.S.C. 242* (death resulting from deprivation of civil rights under color of law)
- *18 U.S.C. 245* (death resulting from deprivation of federally protected activities)
- *18 U.S.C. 247* (death resulting from obstruction of religious beliefs)
- *18 U.S.C. 351* (killing a Member of Congress, cabinet officer, or Supreme Court justice)
- *18 U.S.C. 794* (espionage)
- *18 U.S.C.844(d)* (death resulting from the unlawful transportation of explosives in United States foreign commerce)
- *18 U.S.C. 844(f)* (death resulting from bombing federal property)
- *18 U.S.C. 844(i)* (death resulting from bombing property used in or used in an activity which affects United States foreign commerce)
- *18 U.S.C. 924(c)* (death resulting from carrying or using a firearm during and in relation to a crime of violence or a drug trafficking offense)
- *18 U.S.C.930(c)* (use of a firearm or dangerous weapon a firearm or other dangerous weapon in a federal facility)
- *18 U.S.C.1091* (genocide when the offender is a United States national)
- *18 U.S.C.1111* (murder within the special maritime jurisdiction of the United States)

- *18 U.S.C.1114* (murder of a federal employee, including a member of the United States military, or anyone assisting a federal employee or member of the United States military during the performance of (or on account of) the performance of official duties)
- *18 U.S.C.1116* (murder of an internationally protected person)
- *18 U.S.C.1119* (murder of a U.S. national by another outside the U.S.)
- *18 U.S.C.1120* (murder by a person who has previously escaped from a federal prison)
- *18 U.S.C.1121(a)* (murder of another who is assisting or because of the other's assistance in a federal criminal investigation or killing (because of official status) a state law enforcement officer assisting in a federal criminal investigation)
- *18 U.S.C.1201* (kidnaping where death results)
- *18 U.S.C.1203* (hostage taking where death results)
- *18 U.S.C.1503* (murder to obstruct federal judicial proceedings)
- *18 U.S.C.1512* (tampering with a federal witness or informant where death results)
- *18 U.S.C. 1513* (retaliatory murder of a federal witness or informant)
- *18 U.S.C. 1716* (death resulting from mailing injurious items)
- *18 U.S.C. 1751* (murder of the President, Vice President, or a senior White House official)
- *18 U.S.C. 1958* (murder for hire in violation of U.S. law)
- *18 U.S.C. 1959* (murder in aid of racketeering)
- *18 U.S.C. 1992* (attacks on railroad and mass transit systems engaged in interstate or foreign commerce resulting in death)
- *18 U.S.C. 2113* (murder committed during the course of a bank robbery)
- *18 U.S.C. 2119* (death resulting from carjacking)
- *18 U.S.C.2241, 2245* (aggravated sexual abuse within the special maritime and territorial jurisdiction of the United States where death results)
- *18 U.S.C.2242, 2245* (sexual abuse within the special maritime and territorial jurisdiction of the United States where death results)
- *18 U.S.C.2243, 2245* (sexual abuse of a minor or ward within the special maritime and territorial jurisdiction of the United States where death results)
- *18 U.S.C.2244,2245* (abusive sexual contact within the special maritime and territorial jurisdiction of the United States where death results)
- *18 U.S.C. 2251* (murder during the course of sexual exploitation of a child)

- *18 U.S.C. 2280* (a killing resulting from violence against maritime navigation)
- *18 U.S.C. 2281* (death resulting from violence against fixed maritime platforms)
- *18 U.S.C. 2282A* (murder using devices or dangerous substances in U.S. waters)
- *18 U.S.C. 2283* (transportation of explosives, biological, chemical, radioactive or nuclear materials for terrorist purposes on the high seas or aboard a U.S. vessel or in U.S. waters)
- *18 U.S.C. 2291* (murder in the destruction of vessels or maritime facilities)
- *18 U.S.C. 2332* (killing an American overseas)
- *18 U.S.C. 2332a* (death resulting from use of weapons of mass destruction)
- *18 U.S.C. 2322b* (multinational terrorism involving murder)
- *18 U.S.C. 2332f* (death resulting from bombing of public places, government facilities, public transportation systems or infrastructure facilities)(effective when the terrorist bombing treaty enters into force for the U.S.)
- *18 U.S.C. 2340A* (death resulting from torture committed outside the U.S.)
- *18 U.S.C. 2381* (treason)
- *18 U.S.C. 2441* (war crimes)
- *18 U.S.C. 3261*(murder committed by members of the United States armed forces or accompanying or employed by the United States armed forces overseas)
- *21 U.S.C.461(c)* (murder of federal poultry inspectors during or because of official duties)
- *21 U.S.C.675* (murder of federal meat inspectors during or because of official duties)
- *21 U.S.C. 848(c), 18 U.S.C. 3592b)*(major drug kingpins and attempted murder by drug kingpins to obstruct justice)
- *21 U.S.C.848(e)(1)* (drug kingpin murders)
- *21 U.S.C.1041(c)* (murder of an egg inspector during or because of official duties)
- *42 U.S.C.2283* (killing federal nuclear inspectors during or because of official duties)
- *49 U.S.C. 46502* (air piracy where death results)

- *49 U.S.C.46506* (murder within the special aircraft jurisdiction of the United States)

REFERENCES

[1] As of January 1, 2007, there were 3350 prisoners on death row throughout the United States; 44 of them were there because of a violation of federal law, NAACP Legal Defense Fund, *Death Row USA* 30-1 (Winter, 2007), available on August 31, 2007 at [www.naacpldf.org/content/pdf/pubs/drusa/DRUSA_Winter 2007.pdf].

[2] *See generally* Bazan, *Capital Punishment: An Overview of Federal Death Penalty Statutes*, CRS Rep. RL30962. A list of federal capital offenses is appended.

[3] 18 U.S.C. 3281.

[4] 18 U.S.C. 3235.

[5] 18 U.S.C. 3005.

[6] U.S. Department of Justice, *United States Attorneys Manual*, §§9-10.010 to 9-10.190, available on August 13, 2007 at [www.usdoj.gov/usao/eousa/foia_reading_room/usam].

[7] 18 U.S.C. 3593(a).

[8] 18 U.S.C. 3432.

[9] F.R.Crim.P. 24(b).

[10] 18 U.S.C. 3591-3593.

[11] 18 U.S.C. 3591(a)(1)("A defendant who has been found guilty of – (1) an offense described in section 794 or section 2381 . . . shall be sentenced to death if, after consideration of the factors set forth in section 3592 in the course of a hearing held pursuant to section 3593, it is determined that imposition of a sentence of death is justified, except that no person may be sentenced to death who was less than 18 years of age at the time of the offense").

[12] 18 U.S.C. 3591(a)(2)("any other offense for which a sentence of death is provided, if the defendant, as determined beyond a reasonable doubt at the hearing under section 3593 – (A) intentionally killed the victim; (B) intentionally inflicted serious bodily injury that resulted in the death of the victim; (C) intentionally participated in an act, contemplating that the life of a person would be taken or intending that lethal force would be used in connection with a person, other than one of the participants in the offense, and the victim died as a direct result of the act; or (D) intentionally and

specifically engaged in an act of violence, knowing that the act created a grave risk of death to a person, other than one of the participants in the offense, such that participation in the act constituted a reckless disregard for human life and the victim died as a direct result of the act, shall be sentenced to death if, after consideration of the factors set forth in section 3592 in the course of a hearing held pursuant to section 3593, it is determined that imposition of a sentence of death is justified, except that no person may be sentenced to death who was less than 18 years of age at the time of the offense").

[13] 18 U.S.C. 3591(b)("(b) A defendant who has been found guilty of – (1) an offense referred to in section 408(c)(1) of the Controlled Substances Act (21 U.S.C. 848(c)(1)), committed as part of a continuing criminal enterprise offense under the conditions described in subsection (b) of that section which involved not less than twice the quantity of controlled substance described in subsection (b)(2)(A) or twice the gross receipts described in subsection (b)(2)(B); or (2) an offense referred to in section 408(c)(1) of the Controlled Substances Act (21 U.S.C. 848(c)(1)), committed as part of a continuing criminal enterprise offense under that section, where the defendant is a principal administrator, organizer, or leader of such an enterprise, and the defendant, in order to obstruct the investigation or prosecution of the enterprise or an offense involved in the enterprise, attempts to kill or knowingly directs, advises, authorizes, or assists another to attempt to kill any public officer, juror, witness, or members of the family or household of such a person, shall be sentenced to death if, after consideration of the factors set forth in section 3592 in the course of a hearing held pursuant to section 3593, it is determined that imposition of a sentence of death is justified, except that no person may be sentenced to death who was less than 18 years of age at the time of the offense").

[14] *United States v. Henderson*, 485 F.Supp.2d 831, 871-72 (S.D. Ohio 2007); *United States v. Mayhew*, 380 F.Supp.2d 936, 955-57(S.D. Ohio 2005); *United States v. Johnson*, 362 F.Supp.2d 1043, 1099-111 (N.D. Iowa 2005); *United States v. Jordan*, 357 F.Supp.2d 889, 903-904 (E.D. Va. 2005).

[15] 18 U.S.C. 3592(a)("In determining whether a sentence of death is to be imposed on a defendant, the finder of fact shall consider any mitigating factor, including the following: (1) Impaired capacity.– The defendant's capacity to appreciate the wrongfulness of the defendant's conduct or to conform conduct to the requirements of law was significantly impaired, regardless of whether the capacity was so impaired as to constitute a defense to the charge. (2) Duress.– The defendant was under unusual and

substantial duress, regardless of whether the duress was of such a degree as to constitute a defense to the charge. (3) Minor participation.– The defendant is punishable as a principal in the offense, which was committed by another, but the defendant's participation was relatively minor, regardless of whether the participation was so minor as to constitute a defense to the charge. (4) Equally culpable defendants.– Another defendant or defendants, equally culpable in the crime, will not be punished by death. (5) No prior criminal record.– The defendant did not have a significant prior history of other criminal conduct. (6) Disturbance.– The defendant committed the offense under severe mental or emotional disturbance. (7) Victim's consent.–The victim consented to the criminal conduct that resulted in the victim's death. (8) Other factors.– Other factors in the defendant's background, record, or character or any other circumstance of the offense that mitigate against imposition of the death sentence").

[16] 18 U.S.C. 3592(b), (c), (d) ("The jury, or if there is no jury, the court, may consider whether any other aggravating factor for which notice has been given exists").

[17] 18 U.S.C. 3593(e).

[18] 18 U.S.C. 3592(b).

[19] 18 U.S.C. 3592(c).

[20] 18 U.S.C. 3592(d).

[21] 18 U.S.C. 3593(d)("The jury, or if there is no jury, the court, shall consider all the information received during the hearing. It shall return special findings identifying any aggravating factor or factors set forth in section 3592 found to exist and any other aggravating factor for which notice has been provided under subsection (a) found to exist. A finding with respect to a mitigating factor may be made by 1 or more members of the jury, and any member of the jury who finds the existence of a mitigating factor may consider such factor established for purposes of this section regardless of the number of jurors who concur that the factor has been established. A finding with respect to any aggravating factor must be unanimous. If no aggravating factor set forth in section 3592 is found to exist, the court shall impose a sentence other than death authorized by law").

[22] 18 U.S.C. 3593(e)("If, in the case of – (1) an offense described in section 3591(a)(1), an aggravating factor required to be considered under section 3592(b) is found to exist; (2) an offense described in section 3591(a)(2), an aggravating factor required to be considered under section 3592(c) is found to exist; or (3) an offense described in section 3591(b), an aggravating factor required to be considered under section 3592(d) is found to exist, the

jury, or if there is no jury, the court, shall consider whether all the aggravating factor or factors found to exist sufficiently outweigh all the mitigating factor or factors found to exist to justify a sentence of death, or, in the absence of a mitigating factor, whether the aggravating factor or factors alone are sufficient to justify a sentence of death. Based upon this consideration, the jury by unanimous vote, or if there is no jury, the court, shall recommend whether the defendant should be sentenced to death, to life imprisonment without possibility of release or some other lesser sentence").

[23] U.S. Const. Art. III, §2, cl. 3.

[24] U.S. Const. Amend. VI.

[25] 1 Stat. 88 (1789).

[26] "The trial of offenses punishable with death shall be had in the county where the offense was committed, where that can be done without great inconvenience," 18 U.S.C. 3235.

[27] 35 Stat. 1152 (1909).

[28] "In all cases of murder or manslaughter, the offense shall be deemed to have been committed at the place where the injury was inflicted, or the poison administered or other means employed which caused the death, without regard to the place where the death occurs," 18 U.S.C. 3236.

[29] 14 Stat. 484 (1867).

[30] "(a) Except as otherwise expressly provided by enactment of Congress, any offense against the United States begun in one district and completed in another, or committed in more than one district, may be inquired of and prosecuted in any district in which such offense was begun, continued, or completed. Any offense involving the use of the mails, transportation in interstate or foreign commerce, or the importation of an object or person into the United States is a continuing offense and, except as otherwise expressly provided by enactment of Congress, may be inquired of and prosecuted in any district from, through, or into which such commerce, mail matter, or imported object or person moves," 18 U.S.C. 3237(a). At least one federal appellate court has held that the specific murder-manslaughter instruction of section 3236 overrides the general instructions of section 3237(a) only with regard to "unitary" murder offenses, such as murder by a federal prisoner, *United States v. Barnette*, 211 F.3d 803, 814 (4th Cir. 2000). Section 3236 does not apply, the court held, to "death resulting" cases, cases where murder is a sentencing element rather than a substantive element of the offense, such as in cases of a violation of 18 U.S.C. 924(c)(use of a firearm during and relating to the commission of crime of

violence), the sentence for which is determined in part by whether death resulted from the commission of the offense, *Id.*

[31] "(a) The trial of any offense punishable by death shall be held in the district where the offense was committed or in any district in which the offense began, continued, or was completed. (b) If the offense, or related conduct, under subsection (a) involves activities which affect interstate or foreign commerce, or the importation of an object or person into the United States, such offense may be prosecuted in any district in which those activities occurred," proposed 18 U.S.C. 3235.

[32] The manslaughter features of 3236 presumably continue in place since they are not capital cases and thus by definition are beyond the reach of the proposed capital venue provisions of the amended section 3235.

[33] U.S. Const. Art. III, §2, cl.3; U.S. Const. Amend. VI.

[34] 524 U.S. 1, 7-10 (1998)("The money laundering counts included no act committed by Cabrales in Missouri. . . nor did the government charge that Cabrales transported the money from Missouri to Florida. . . . [T]he counts at issue do not charge Cabrales with conspiracy; they do not link her to, or assert her responsibility for, acts done by others. . . . In the counts at issue, the government indicted Cabrales for transactions which began, continued, and were completed only in Florida").

[35] 524 U.S. at 8, 10.

[36] 526 U.S. at 280 (emphasis added).

[37] 526 U.S. at 280-82.

[38] 526 U.S. at 280-81 n.4. The Court declined to address, however, the so-called "effects" test used by the some of the lower federal courts in obstruction of justice and Hobbs Act ("effect") cases to determine the presence of proper venue, 526 U.S. at 279 n.2.

[39] *United States v. Smith*, 452 F.3d 323, 335 (4th Cir. 2006)("venue on a count is proper only in a district in which an essential conduct element of the offense takes place"); *United States v. Clenney*, 434 F.3d 780, 782 (5th Cir. 2005); *United States v. Ramirez*, 420 F.3d 134, 139 (2d Cir. 2005); *United States v. Salinas*, 373 F.3d 161, 164 (1st Cir. 2004); *United States v. Morgan*, 393 F.3d 192, 196 (D.C.Cir. 2004)(internal citations and quotation marks omitted) ("When the statute proscribing the offense does not contain an express venue provision, the *locus delicti* must be determined from the nature of the crime alleged and the location of the act or acts constituting it"); *United States v. Wood*, 364 F.3d 704, 711 (6th Cir. 2004); *United States v. Breitweiser*, 357 F.3d 1249, 1253 (11th Cir. 2004). Congress may not bring into effect an express statutory provision in contravention of

constitutional demands, but it may limit the choice of venue where the Constitution permits trial in more than one place, and it may define the place of trial from crimes committed outside any of the states, U.S.Const. Art. III, §2, cl.3.

[40] Proposed 18 U.S.C. 3235.

[41] *E.g.*, *United States v. Zidell*, 323 F.3d 412, 422 (6th Cir. 2003)(possession with intent to distribute); *United States v. Brown*, 400 F.3d 1242, 1250 (10th Cir. 2005)(manufacturing methamphetamine).

[42] "Whoever, as consideration for the receipt of, or as consideration for a promise or agreement to pay, anything of pecuniary value from an enterprise engaged in racketeering activity, or for the purpose of gaining entrance to or maintaining or increasing position in an enterprise engaged in racketeering activity, murders, kidnaps, maims, assaults with a dangerous weapon, commits assault resulting in serious bodily injury upon, or threatens to commit a crime of violence against any individual in violation of the laws of any State or the United States, or attempts or conspires so to do, shall be punished – . . ." 18 U.S.C. 1959(a).

[43] Proposed 18 U.S.C. 1959(c).

[44] *United States v. Saaverdra*, 223 F.3d 85, 91-2 (2d Cir. 2000); *see also United States v. Williams*, 181 F.Supp.2d 267, 290-92 (S.D.N.Y. 2001).

[45] 18 U.S.C. 3005.

[46] *Id.* ("Whoever is indicted for treason or other capital crime shall be allowed to make his full defense by counsel; and the court before which the defendant is to be tried, or a judge thereof, shall promptly, upon the defendant's request, assign 2 such counsel . . . "); *In re Sterling-Suarez*, 306 F.3d 1170, 1173 (1st Cir. 2002)(". . . counsel is to be appointed reasonably soon after the indictment and prior to the time that submissions are to be made to persuade the Attorney General not to seek the death penalty").

[47] *United States v. Boone*, 245 F.3d 352, 359-61(4th Cir. 2001)(right exists regardless of whether the government decides to seek the death penalty); *contra*, *United States v. Waggoner*, 339 F.3d 915, 917 (9th Cir. 2003)("the district court properly concluded that the defendant was not entitled to be represented by two attorneys after the government filed formal notice that it did not intend to seek the death penalty"); *cf.*, *United States v. Casseus*, 282 F.3d 253, 256 (3d Cir. 2002)("the purpose of 18 U.S.C. 3005 is to allow a capital defendant to 'make his full defense by counsel.' This, they were fully able to do. Moreover, after the government declared that it would not seek the death penalty, the appellants were no longer capital defendants").

[48] Hearing at 14-5 ("Because there is no procedural difference between the trial of a non-capital offense and the non-death penalty trial of a capital offense, it is clear that the appointment of learned capital counsel was intended to provide a defendant with the assistance of a second counsel in a death penalty prosecution. Despite the clear intent to provide additional assistance to defendants in death penalty prosecutions, the Fourth Circuit has construed the existing provisions of section 3005 in such a way as to require a trial court to retain capital counsel through the conclusion of the trial – even in those cases in which the Attorney General decides not to seek the death penalty. . . Second, the courts have not infrequently complained about the expenditure of resources in providing expert capital counsel in cases in which, in a court's view, a death penalty prosecution is unlikely. Currently, the right to second, learned capital counsel adheres upon indictment for a capital offense. Courts outside the Fourth Circuit have construed this to require the assistance of expert counsel only until there is as decision not to seek the death penalty")(Griffey statement).

[49] Proposed 18 U.S.C. 3005(a).

[50] *Death Penalty Reform Act of 2006: Hearing Before the Subcomm. on Crime, Terrorism, and Homeland Security of the House Comm. on the Judiciary*, 109th Cong., 2d Sess. (Hearing), 44 (prepared statement of David L. Bruck, Federal Death Penalty Resource Counsel, Clinical Professor of Law and Director, Virginia Capital Case Clearinghouse, Washington and Lee School of Law)(Bruck statement), quoting in *In re Sterling-Suarez*, 306 F.3d at 1175 ("In some cases the early appointment of learned counsel . . . may well make the difference as to whether the Attorney General seeks the death penalty. . . where the opposition succeeds in persuading the Attorney General not to seek the death penalty, a substantial additional expenditure on the trial and sentencing phase of the as capital case is like to be avoided").

[51] 18 U.S.C. 3593(a)("If, in a case involving an offense described in section 3591, the attorney for the government believes that the circumstances of the offense are such that a sentence of death is justified under this chapter, the attorney shall, a reasonable time before the trial or before acceptance by the court of a plea of guilty, sign and file with the court, and serve on the defendant, a notice – (1) stating that the government believes that the circumstances of the offense are such that, if the defendant is convicted, a sentence of death is justified under this chapter and that the government will seek the sentence of death; and (2) setting forth the aggravating factor or

factors that the government, if the defendant is convicted, proposes to prove as justifying a sentence of death").

[52] *United States v. Ferebe*, 332 F.3d 722 (4th Cir. 2003); *United States v. Wilk*, 452 F.3d 1208 (11th Cir. 2006); *see also United States v. Ayala-Loopez*, 457 F.3d 107, 108 (1st Cir. 2006)(assuming with some reservations that interlocutory appeal was available, but concluding that the defendant had been given timely notice).

[53] *United States v. Robinson*, 473 F.3d 487, 491-92 (2d Cir. 2007).

[54] Hearing at 12-3 ("All agree that the defendant must be put on notice in a timely manner of the government's intention to seek the death penalty. Unfortunately, in *United States v. Ferebe*, 332 F.3d 722 (4th Cir. 2003), the Fourth Circuit concluded that the determination of whether a notice of intent has been filed in a timely manner must be made with respect the trial date in effect at the time the notice is filed and without regard to the additional preparation and issues resulting from a death penalty prosecution. In other words in the Fourth Circuit, an actual trial date cannot be continued to allow the defense adequate time to prepare for the capital punishment hearing. Particularly in those courts with what is know[n] as a 'rocket docket,' the *Ferebe* rule could result in the dismissal of a death notice. In some instances, in order not to forfeit the ability to seek a death sentence, the Department has been forced to file a 'protective death notice.' A 'protective death notice' is one that is filed in a case before the case has been fully reviewed and the Attorney General has made a final decision whether or not to seek the death penalty. In cases in which the Attorney General decides not to seek the death penalty, the protective notice is then withdrawn. The Department of Justice is committed to the goal of the consistent, fair and even-handed application of the death penalty, regardless of geography and local sentiment. The decision whether it is appropriate to seek the death penalty involves awesome responsibilities and consequences. The *Ferebe* court's understanding of the existing section 3593(a) provisions favors expedience over considered decision-making, and when a considered decision cannot be reached in a limited amount of time, it forces the government to choose between filing a protective death notice or abandoning the goal of consistency and evenhandedness in the application of the death penalty")(Griffey statement).

[55] "(a) Notice by the government.– If, in a case involving an offense described in section 3591, the attorney for the government believes that the circumstances of the offense are such that a sentence of death is justified under this chapter, the attorney shall, a reasonable time before the trial or

before acceptance by the court of a plea of guilty, sign and file with the court, and serve on the defendant, a notice – (1) stating that the government believes that the circumstances of the offense are such that, if the defendant is convicted, a sentence of death is justified under this chapter and that the government will seek the sentence of death; and (2) setting forth the aggravating factor or factors that the government, if the defendant is convicted, proposes to prove as justifying a sentence of death. *The notice must be filed a reasonable time before trial or before acceptance by the court of a plea of guilty. The court shall, where necessary to ensure adequate preparation time for the defense, grant a reasonable continuance of the trial. If the government has not filed a notice of intent to seek the death penalty or informed the court that a notice of intent to seek the death penalty will not be filed, the court shall not accept a plea of guilty to an offense described in section 3591 without the concurrence of the government. . .* " Proposed 18 U.S.C. 3593 with deleted language struck out and additional language in italics.

[56] Proposed 18 U.S.C. 3593(b)(1)("*(1) If, as required under subsection (a), the government has filed notice seeking a sentence of death, the defendant shall, a reasonable time before the trial, sign and file with the court and serve on the attorney for the government, notice setting forth the mitigating factor or factors that the defendant proposes to prove mitigate against imposition of a sentence of death. . .*").

[57] Proposed 18 U.S.C. 3593(a).

[58] Proposed 18 U.S.C. 3593(b)(3)("*Following the filing of a defendant's notice under this subsection, the court shall, where necessary to ensure adequate preparation time for the government, grant a reasonable continuance of the trial*").

[59] Hearing at 42 ("While this proposal has a superficially attractive symmetry to the government's obligation to provide pre-trial notice of aggravating factors, it overlooks the real differences between aggravation and mitigation. Most importantly, an across-the-board notice requirement for defendants would effectively require many defendants to acknowledge factual guilt before trial, and would thus be unconstitutional. A defendant cannot personally 'sign' and file notice of intent to provide a mitigating factor (such as having committed the offense under duress, or under the influence of extreme emotional disturbance) without admitting guilt of the underlying offense. That is why, to my knowledge, no state death penalty statute requires this kind of broad pre-trial notice of mitigating factors, and

why this provision would be unenforceable under the Fifth Amendment")(Bruck statement).

[60] *Atkins v. Virginia*, 536 U.S. 304, 318 (2002)("Mentally retarded persons frequently know the difference between right and wrong and are competent to stand trial").

[61] 18 U.S.C. 3592(a)("In determining whether a sentence of death is to be imposed on a defendant, the finder of fact shall consider any mitigating factor, including the following: (1) Impaired capacity.– The defendant's capacity to appreciate the wrongfulness of the defendant's conduct or to conform conduct to the requirements of law was significantly impaired, regardless of whether the capacity was so impaired as to constitute a defense to the charge. . . (6) Disturbance.– The defendant committed the offense under severe mental or emotional disturbance. . .(8) Other factors.– Other factors in the defendant's background, record, or character or any other circumstance of the offense that mitigate against imposition of the death sentence"); *United States v. Cisneros*, 385 F.Supp.2d 567 (E.D.Va. 2005).

[62] *Atkins v. Virginia*, 536 U.S. 304, 321 (2002); 18 U.S.C. 3596(c).

[63] *United States v. Nelson*, 419 F.Supp.2d 891, 892-94 (E.D.La. 2006); *United States v. Sablan*, 461 F.Supp.2d 1239, 1240-243 (D.Colo. 2006); *but see United States v. Cisneros*, 385 F.Supp.2d 567, 571 (E.D.Va. 2005)(agreeing with the preponderance standard but concluding that the question should be handled by the jury following conviction with the understanding that if unanimous the death penalty might not be imposed and if found by fewer than twelve of the jurors considered as mitigation).

[64] "The American Association on Mental Retardation (AAMR) defines mental retardation as follows: '*Mental retardation* refers to substantial limitations in present functioning. It is characterized by significantly subaverage intellectual functioning, existing concurrently with related limitations in two or more of the following applicable adaptive skill areas: communication, self-care, home living, social skills, community use, self-direction, health and safety, functional academics, leisure, and work. Mental retardation manifests before age 18' Mental Retardation: Definition, Classification, and Systems of Supports 5 (9th ed.1992). The American Psychiatric Association's definition is similar: 'The essential feature of Mental Retardation is significantly subaverage general intellectual functioning (Criterion A) that is accompanied by significant limitations in adaptive functioning in at least two of the following skill areas: communication, self-care, home living, social/ interpersonal skills, use of community resources,

self-direction, functional academic skills, work, leisure, health, and safety (Criterion B). The onset must occur before age 18 years (Criterion C). Mental Retardation has many different etiologies and may be seen as a final common pathway of various pathological processes that affect the functioning of the central nervous system.' Diagnostic and Statistical Manual of Mental Disorders 41 (4th ed.2000). 'Mild' mental retardation is typically used to describe people with an IQ level of 50-55 to approximately 70. *Id.*, at 42-43," 536 U.S. at 308 n.3.

[65] Proposed 18 U.S.C. 3593(b)(1)("*(1) If, as required under subsection (a), the government has filed notice seeking a sentence of death, the defendant shall, a reasonable time before the trial, sign and file with the court and serve on the attorney for the government, notice setting forth the mitigating factor or factors that the defendant proposes to prove mitigate against imposition of a sentence of death. . .*").

[66] Proposed 18 U.S.C. 3593(b)(1)("(1) . . . *In any case in which the defendant intends to raise the issue of mental retardation as precluding a sentence of death, the defendant shall, a reasonable time before trial, sign and file with the court, and serve on the attorney for the government, notice of such intent*)."

[67] Proposed 18 U.S.C. 3593(b)(2), (3) ("*(2) When a defendant makes a claim of mental retardation or intends to rely on evidence of mental impairment, or other mental defect or disease as a mitigating factor under this section, the government shall have the right to an independent mental health examination of the defendant. A mental health examination ordered under this subsection shall be conducted by a licensed and certified psychiatrist, psychologist, neurologist, psychopharamacologist, or other allied mental health professional. If the court finds it appropriate, more than one such professional shall perform the examination. To facilitate the examination, the court may commit the person to be examined for a reasonable period, not to exceed 30 days to the custody of the Attorney General for placement in a suitable facility. Unless impracticable, the psychiatric or psychological examination shall be conducted in a suitable facility reasonably close to the court. The director of the facility may apply for a reasonable extension, but not to exceed 15 days upon a showing of good cause that the additional time is necessary to observe and evaluate the defendant. (3) Following the filing of a defendant's notice under this subsection, the court shall, where necessary to ensure adequate preparation time for the government, grant a reasonable continuance of the trial*").

[68] Proposed 18 U.S.C. 3593(d)("(*d*) Proof of mitigating and aggravating factors. – . . . The defendant may present any information relevant to a mitigating factor *for which notice has been provided under subsection (b). If the defendant has raised the issue of mental retardation as required under subsection (b), the defendant may introduce information relevant to mental retardation.. .* "). The caption ("proof of mitigating and aggravating factors") could be read to mean that the provisions are not intended to apply to the statutory and constitutional bars to execution. The articulation of separate burden of proof provisions for first mitigating factors and then mental retardation issues, quoted below, renders such an interpretation more uncertain.

[69] Proposed 18 U.S.C. 3593(d)("(*d*). . .The burden of establishing the existence of any mitigating factor is on the defendant, and is not satisfied unless the existence of such a factor is established by a preponderance of the information. *The defendant shall have the burden of proving mental retardation by the preponderance of the information*").

[70] Proposed 18 U.S.C. 3593(e)("(*e*) Return of special findings.– . . . *In any case in which the defendant has raised the issue of mental retardation as required under subsection (b), the jury, or if there is no jury, the court, shall determine the issue of mental retardation only if any aggravating factor set forth in section 3592 is found to exist. Such determination shall occur prior to the consideration of any mitigating factor. . .*").

[71] Proposed 18 U.S.C. 3593(e)("(*e*) Return of special findings.– . . . If no aggravating factor set forth in section 3592 is found to exist, the court shall impose a sentence other than death authorized by law. *If the jury, or if there is no jury, the court, determines that the defendant is mentally retarded, the court shall sentence the defendant to life imprisonment without the possibility of release, or some other lesser sentence authorized by law.*

[72] Proposed 18 U.S.C. 3593(b)(4)("*(b)(4) For purposes of this section, a defendant is mentally retarded if, since some point in time prior to age 18, he or she has continuously had an intelligence quotient of 70 or lower and, as a result of that significant subaverage mental functioning, has since that point in time continuously had a diminished capacity to understand and process information, abstract from mistakes and learn from experience, engage in logical reasoning, control impulses, and understand others' reactions*").

[73] Hearing at 12 (Griffey statement).

[74] Hearing at 39-40 ("The procedures proposed. . . fall well short of *Atkins* constitutional minimum , and would thus contravene the Eight

Amendment." The language of proposed 18 U.S.C. 3593(b)(4) "is not a definition at all, but rather a listing of many of the characteristics of people with mental retardation that the *Atkins* Court regarded as justifying a categorical bar against the infliction of death upon such defendants. In effect, this provision would require the jury to redetermine anew in each case whether the Supreme Court was correct in *Atkins* when it found that these characteristics of mental retardation justified a categorical exemption. Note that the provision requires the jury to find *all* of the listed characteristics (and that all these characteristics have manifested themselves 'continuously' since some point prior to age 18) in order to exempt a defendant on grounds of mental retardation. Thus, a defendant with an IQ of 70 or below who established, for example, that he had 'diminished capacity to understand and process information, abstract from mistakes and learn from experience, engage in logical reasoning, [and] control impulses,' but who did *not* establish that he also had diminished capacity to 'understand others' reactions' would have failed to establish mental retardation, and could therefore be executed. It can readily be seen that this approach fails to protect the entire class of persons with mental retardation, and enactment would therefore place the federal government in violation of the Eighth Amendment rule of *Atkins*. Indeed, the whole point of the Supreme Court's decision in *Atkins* was that each of the acts of moral culpability was too difficult to determine reliable on a case-by-case basis, and the severity of the disability suffered by all persons with mental retardation (whose intellectual functioning places them, by definition, in the bottom 2-3 percent of the population) justifies a categorical ban")(Bruck statement).

[75] *Id.* at 41 ("The procedures to be employed are also undesirable. Rather than a pretrial judicial determination (as occurs with competency to stand trial, for example, *see* 18 U.S.C. 4241)," the bills "would wastefully require a defendant with mental retardation to go through the entire elaborate structure of a capital trial(with special jury selection procedures, bifurcated jury sentencing, special counsel provisions, and so forth), only to establish at the end of the process that he suffered all along from a life-long disability that rendered moot the entire death-penalty aspect of the proceedings – and that could have been determined at the start. Because mental retardation (unlike mental illness) is an essentially fixed condition that must have existed prior to age 18 and that does not resolve or dissipate over time, it is obviously more efficient and more logical to determine this issue before trial rather than at the end of the proceedings. Almost all state statutes implementing mental retardation bars in death penalty proceedings adopt

this approach. . . Delaying the jury's mental retardation verdict until *after* the presentation of aggravation evidence is also unfair, because it ensures that the jury will not address the relatively straightforward issues of whether the defendant meets the clinical definition of mental retardation until it has been overwhelmed with inflammatory information about the defendant's prior record and bad character and with emotionally powerful victim impact evidence. Just as it has long been thought unfair to present sentencing evidence (including evidence of prior offenses and bad character) to a jury before the defendant's *guilt* or innocent has been determined, so too is it unfair to delay a determination of whether the defendant has the immutable disability of mental retardation until all of the evidence that might make the jury wish to impose the death penalty –retardation or no retardation – has been presented")(Bruck statement).

[76] *Id.* at 42 ("[T]he proposed 18 U.S.C. 3593(b)(1) and (2) set up a partial new procedure for pre-trial rebuttal mental heath evaluations in capital cases without taking into account the detailed set of procedures that only recently went into effect with the December 2002 amendments to rule 12.2, Fed. R.Crim.P. Rule 12.2 already requires written pre-trial notice of expert mental health mitigation testimony, and authorizes government rebuttal evaluations following such notice. Adding on a statutory provision that is much less detailed than Rule 12.2 is likely to cause confusion, while adding little or nothing to the government's valid entitlement to a fair opportunity to rebut the defendant's mitigation"). (Bruck statement). The text of Rule 12.2 is appended.

[77] Proposed 18 U.S.C. 3592(a)(4).

[78] Hearing at 46 ("To be sure, a strong argument can be made that the hypothetical defendant described here might still cite the disparate punishments in their cases as a nonstatutory mitigating factor. In all likelihood, however, some federal courts would construe Congress's enactment of this amendment as intended to preclude reliance on such mitigating factors, while other courts would allow it")(Bruck statement).

[79] Proposed 18 U.S.C. 3592(b)(4)("In determining whether a sentence of death is justified for an offense described in section 3591(a)(1)[espionage and treason], the jury, or if there is no jury, the court, shall consider each of the following aggravating factors for which notice has been given and determine which, if any, exist: . . (4) Substantial planning – The defendant committed the offense after substantial planning").

[80] 1 Stat. 112 (1796).

[81] *See*, *Coker v. Georgia*, 433 U.S. 584, 598 (1977)("We have the abiding conviction that the death penalty . . . is an excessive penalty for the rapist who, as such, does not take human life")(holding that the death penalty may not be imposed for the rape of an adult woman even when committed by a defendant previously sentenced to three consecutive life terms for an earlier murder and two earlier rapes).

[82] Proposed 18 U.S.C. 3592(c)(1)("In determining whether a sentence of death is justified for an offense described in section 3591(a)(2)[homicide], the jury, or if there is no jury, the court, shall consider each of the following aggravating factors for which notice has been given and determine which, if any, exist: (1) Death during commission of another crime.–The death, or injury resulting in death, occurred during the commission or attempted commission of, or during the immediate flight from the commission of, an offense under section . . .2339D (terrorist offenses resulting in death) . . . ").

[83] Proposed 18 U.S.C. 3592(c)(1). H.R. 1914 (Rep. Carter) inserts section 2339E offenses into section 3592(c)(1). There is no section under 2339E in existing law and H.R. 1914 does not create one. S. 1860 (Sen. Cornyn) and H.R. 3156 (Rep. Lamar Smith) do create a section 2339E (terrorist offenses resulting in death), but neither bill adds the new section to section 3592(c)(1).

[84] Hearing at 16-7 ("The death penalty is and should be reserved for appropriate circumstances and the 'worst of the worst' offenders. Examples of appropriate circumstances include those in which individuals put multiple lives at risk or threaten the integrity of our judicial system. Currently, however, these circumstances are not always death-penalty-eligible")(prepared statement of Margaret P. Griffey, Chief, Capital Case Unit, United States Department of Justice)(Griffey statement).

[85] Hearing at 33-34 ("The jury can already consider all relevant sentencing factors as nonstatutory aggravation. . . Rather, the point of creating a new statutory aggravating factor is to authorize the jury to impose the death penalty *on that basis alone*, when no other statutory aggravating factor is present. Since the FDPA's existing list of statutory aggravating factors already includes some 35 separate bases for death eligibility, some of them extremely broad (such as that the murder was committed after 'substantial planning and premeditation'), the only practical effect of adding still more factors is to make the death penalty available in that small category of cases where the murder was not otherwise aggravated. . . . Once the effect of such new death-eligibility factors is properly understood, one might expect some actual showing of a need to further expand the list of death-eligible federal

murders before adding more death-eligibility factors to this already long list")(emphasis in the original)(Bruck statement).

[86] Proposed 18 U.S.C. 3592(c)(17)("In determining whether a sentence of death is justified for an offense described in section 3591(a)(2)[homicide], the jury, or if there is no jury, the court, shall consider each of the following aggravating factors for which notice has been given and determine which, if any, exist: . . . (17) Obstruction of Justice – The defendant engaged in any conduct resulting in the death of another person in order to obstruct the investigation or prosecution of any offense").

[87] Hearing at 22 (prepared statement of Robert Steinbuch, Professor of Law, University of Arkansas); 19 ("The Department further supports the addition of new statutory aggravator related to obstruction of justice. Protecting the integrity of te justice system is a paramount goal for the Department")(Griffiey statement).

[88] Hearing at 36-7 ("Moreover, even if language were added to make clear that the proposed 'obstruction of justice' factor requires some nexus to the capital homicide offense at issue, the new factor would still be susceptible of very broad application, because it could be construed to apply to any murder committed to avoid arrest. If so construed, such a relatively uncontroversial-seeming expansion of the federal death penalty could eliminate almost every remaining murder under federal jurisdiction that is not currently subject to the death penalty. That is, this provision could remove the last bit of legislative 'narrowing' from the FDPA, leaving the decision to inflict or withhold death to the unfettered discretion of the jury in every case. Eventually the Supreme Court may take up the question of whether a given capital punishment statute has become so all-inclusive that it fails the basic requirement of *Furman* and *Gregg* that the sentencer's discretion be legislatively narrowed and guided")(Bruck statement).

[89] 18 U.S.C. 924(j).

[90] Hearing at 18 ("As currently worded, the factor is susceptible to two interpretations, which could undermine the clear and consistent application of the factor. Under one interpretation, a prior conviction for an offense involving a firearm could constitute an aggravating factor for all capital offenses except those involving firearms, an illogical interpretation considering that a defendant's prior firearm conviction may be relevant when the same defendant's later use of a firearm has resulted in death. The other interpretation would only prohibit basing the aggravating factor on the immediately-prior section 924(j) conviction for which the defendant faces the death penalty"). This second interpretation seems to be the more faithful

reading of the statute. Nevertheless. a third interpretation possible: An earlier firearms conviction under any law other than section 924(c) may be considered as an aggravating factor, but a section 924(c) conviction may not be used as an aggravating factor regardless whether the conviction is the occasion of the current sentencing proceeding or occurred sometime previously.

[91] Proposed 18 U.S.C. 3592(c)(2)("For any offense, other than an offense for which a sentence of death is sought on the basis of section 924(c), The defendant has previously *in a prior adjudication* been convicted of a Federal or State offense punishable by a term of imprisonment of more than 1 year, involving the use or attempted or threatened use of a firearm (as defined in section 921) against another person").

[92] Hearing at 35-6 ("The reason Congress enacted the 924(c) exclusion in the firearms aggravator, 18 U.S.C. 3592(c)(2), was to avoid making every firearm killing automatically death-eligible. This would otherwise have occurred because the firearms violation that serves as the predicate for the 924(j) conviction would do double-duty as a 'prior conviction' of a 'prior' qualifying firearms offense. By removing this exemption now, Congress would seemingly be making every federal firearms killing death-eligible, whether or not it would be otherwise warranted. In other words, there would be no requirement that the defendant have any genuinely prior record, and without requiring evidence of any other aggravating factor (such as substantial planning and premeditation, risk to additional persons, multiple victims, cruelty or torture, etc. . .The enactment of 18 U.S.C. 924(j) in 1994 represented a potentially enormous expansion in federal jurisdiction over homicide offenses, which from the founding of the nation have been primarily a matter for state law enforcement. The §924(c) exclusion at least represented an effort to keep this huge change under some sort of commonsense check by ensuring that every 924(j) offense would not automatically become punishable by death in the unfettered discretion of the jury. Removing this restraint is unwise, unnecessary (because any truly aggravated 924(j) killing is already death-eligible under existing law), and open to constitutional challenge as impermissibly all-inclusive under the two seminal Supreme Court cases governing capital punishment law, *Furman v. Georgia* and *Gregg v. Georgia*")(Bruck statement).

[93] *Cf., United States v. Walker*, 901 F.Supp. 837, 848-49 (N.D.N.Y. 1995)(interpreting comparable language then found in the drug capital punishment provisions of 21 U.S.C. 848)(Section "848(n)(7) [has] two separate prongs: the first 'as consideration for' language contemplates only

murder-for-hire, but the 'in expectation of' language identifies a separate ground").

[94] *United States v. Barnette*, 390 F.3d 775, 805-807 (4th Cir. 2004), *vac'd and remanded on other grounds*, 546 U.S. 803 (2005)("Both the Fifth Circuit and Tenth Circuit have limited the application of the pecuniary gain aggravating factor 'to situations where the murder itself was committed as consideration for, or in the expectation of, anything of pecuniary value.' *United States v. Bernard*, 299 F.3d 467, 483 (5th Cir. 2002)(quoting *United States v. Chanthadara*, 230 F.3d 1237, 1263 (10th Cir. 2000)) . . . The defendants in *Bernard* carjacked a vehicle and robbed the owners. . . drove the vehicle for several hours with the couple in the truck, and [then] murdered the couple. . . .[T]he Fifth Circuit concluded that the motivation for the murders was not pecuniary gain but was instead to prevent the couple from reporting the crime to the police. . . Chanthadara argued that §3592(c)(8) was inapplicable because all of the valuable property in the restaurant had been [stolen] by the defendant and his accomplices prior to the killing. The Tenth Circuit agreed. . .Unlike *Bernard*, the evidence in the instant case was sufficient for the jury to conclude that Barnette killed Allen in the expectation of the receipt of something of pecuniary value, namely Allen's vehicle"); *United States v. Roman*, 371 F.Supp.2d 36, 46 (D.P.R. 2005)("Under these facts, a finding of pecuniary gain would not involve an extension of existing law. A jury could properly infer that the murder was committed for the express reason to effect the robbery, rather than being incident to, or as an afterthought to the robbery").

[95] Hearing at 18-9 ("As now interpreted by the courts, the pecuniary-gain aggravating factor applies when the murder, as viewed by the defendant, is necessary to initially secure the security gain, but does not apply when committed to maintain possession of a stolen gain. Thus, for example, courts have held the factor to be applicable when a carjacking victim is killed at a dark intersection before the vehicle is taken but not applicable if the carjacking occurs in a public setting and the victim is taken a few miles away before he is killed") (Griffey statement).

[96] Proposed 18 U.S.C. 3592(c)(17)("In determining whether a sentence of death is justified for an offense described in section 3591(a)(2)[homicide], the jury, or if there is no jury, the court, shall consider each of the following aggravating factors for which notice has been given and determine which, if any, exist: . . . (17) Killing of law enforcement officer – The defendant killed or attempted to kill a person who is authorized by law to engage in or supervise the prevention, detention, investigation, or prosecution of any

criminal violation of law; or to arrest or prosecute an individual for any such violation").

[97] 18 U.S.C. 3592(c)(14)(D)("The defendant committed the offense against . ..(D) a Federal public servant who is a judge, a law enforcement officer, or an employee of a United States penal or correctional institution – (i) while he or she is engaged in the performance of his or her official duties; (ii) because of the performance of his or her official duties; or (iii) because of his or her status as a public servant. For purposes of this subparagraph, a "law enforcement officer" is a public servant authorized by law or by a Government agency or Congress to conduct or engage in the prevention, investigation, or prosecution or adjudication of an offense, and includes those engaged in corrections, parole, or probation functions").

[98] 479 U.S. 538, 539-43 (1987).

[99] Proposed 18 U.S.C. 3593(f)("*(f) . . . In assessing the appropriateness of a sentence of death, the jury, or if there is no jury, the court must base the decision on the facts of the offense and the aggravating and mitigating factors and avoid any influence of sympathy sentiment, passion, prejudice, or other arbitrary factor when imposing sentence. . .* ").

[100] Proposed 18 U.S.C. 3593(e)(". . . . *In assessing the appropriateness of a sentence of death, the jury, or if there is no jury, the court must base the decision on the facts of the offense and the aggravating and mitigating factors and avoid any influence of passion, prejudice, or other arbitrary factor when imposing sentence. . . .*").

[101] Hearing at 43 ("The evident purpose of this provision would be to allow the government to seek a jury instruction using this verbiage. However, instructing a capital sentencing jury to avoid 'any influence' of sympathy when choosing between life and death runs a grave risk of violating the constitutional requirement of *Lockett v. Ohio*, 438 U.S. 586 (1978) and *Eddings v. Oklahoma*, 455 U.S. 104 (1982), that the sentencer consider all relevant mitigating evidence before imposing death as [a] punishment. I realize that in *California v. Brown*, 479 U.S. 538 (1987), the Supreme Court narrowly upheld a rather different instruction not to be swayed by 'mere sentiment, conjecture, sympathy, or sympathy. . .' However, the language proposed here is much more sweeping. It is simply impossible to reconcile a prohibition of 'any influence of sympathy' with the constitutional directive to consider the kinds of mitigating evidence – including horrific childhood abuse, or severe mental and physical disabilities – which tend to elicit sympathy by their very nature. There is no reason to push the constitutional envelope in order to help the government persuade jurors to stifle their own

sympathetic responses to those 'compassionate or mitigating factors stemming from the diverse frailties of humankind' which must be considered 'as a constitutionally indispensable part of the process of inflicting the penalty of death.' *Woodson v. North Carolina*, 428 U.S. 280, 304 (1976)(opinion of Stewart, Powell, and Stevens, JJ.). This amendment is unnecessary, unwise, and unconstitutional")(Bruck statement).

[102] *E.g.*, 18 U.S.C. 1111(b)(murder in the special maritime and territorial jurisdiction of the United States).

[103] *E.g.*, 18 U.S.C. 844(h)(use of fire or explosives in the commission of a federal offense); 924(j)(use of a firearm during and in relation to a crime of violence or drug trafficking crime).

[104] 18 U.S.C. 3592(d).

[105] 18 U.S.C. 3592(e).

[106] Proposed 18 U.S.C. 3592(f), 3594.

[107] 18 U.S.C. 3593(b).

[108] Proposed 18 U.S.C. 3593(c).

[109] Hearing at 47 ("Fed.R.Crim.P. 23(b) currently authorizes an 11-member jury to return a verdict where one juror is dismissed for good cause, even without the defendant's consent or stipulation. This provision presumably already applies to capital as well as non-capital cases." The proposed amendment "would apply this to re-sentencing juries in capital cases, but in so doing would remove the 11-juror minimum , thus allowing for even smaller juries – of virtually any size – so long as the judge finds good cause for dismissing two or more jurors. Even more significantly, this provision clearly authorizes judges to empanel resentencing juries of less than 12 members – with no apparent minimum number – so long as undefined 'good cause' is found to exist. I am not aware of any justification for so radical a potential departure from the centuries-old practice of requiring 12-member juries in capital cases, and do not think that Congress should enact it without a very powerful justification being shown")(Bruck statement).

[110] Proposed F.R.Crim.P. 24(c)(1), (4).

[111] Proposed 18 U.S.C. 3593(c)("*(c)* ... *The court shall not dismiss alternate jurors impaneled during the guilt phase unless for good cause as to individual alternates or upon a finding, under this subsection, that the sentencing hearing will be heard by the court alone. The court shall retain such alternate jurors to hear the sentencing trial until the completion of the hearing. If at any time, whether before or after the final submission of the sentencing case to the jury, a sitting juror dies or becomes ill, or upon other good cause shown to the court is found to be unable to perform his or her*

duty in a timely manner, or if a juror requests a discharge and good cause appears therefor, the court shall order the juror to be discharged and draw the name of an alternate, who shall then take a place in the jury box, and be subject to the same rules and regulations as though the alternate juror had been selected as one of the original jurors. If deliberations have begun when the substitution is made, the court shall instruct the newly constituted jury to recommence deliberations as if none had previously taken place. The panel, in all other respects, shall be considered unaltered by the substitution of a duly seated alternate").

[112] Proposed 18 U.S.C. 3593(b)("The court shall retain alternate jurors until the completion of the sentencing hearing, unless the sentencing is before the court alone under paragraph (3). The replacement of jurors with alternate jurors during the sentencing hearing will be conducted in accordance with Rule 24 of the Rules of Criminal Procedure").

[113] 18 U.S.C. 3593(e).

[114] 18 U.S.C. 3594.

[115] Proposed 18 U.S.C. 3593(b)((2)(E).

[116] 18 U.S.C. 3597, 3596.

[117] Proposed 18 U.S.C. 3597, 3596.

[118] Hearing at 16 ("Prior to the establishment of the federal death row in Terre Haute, and the building of an execution facility there, it was necessary for federal death-sentenced inmates to be housed in state facilities and, it was anticipated executed under state procedures. Existing statutes reflect this practice and expectation. As it turns out, the federal facility was in place prior to the first federal execution. There is therefore no reason to continue to provide courts with the option of designating a state facility or method of execution ass applicable in a particular case, particularly as this state of affairs can create uncertainty")(Griffey statement)

[119] Proposed 18 U.S.C. 3597(c).

[120] "(a) Whoever, during a presidentially-declared major disaster or emergency – (1) forcibly assaults, resists, opposes, impedes, intimidates, or interferes with any officer or employee of the United States or of any agency in any branch of the United States Government (including any member of the uniformed services while such officer or employee is engaged in or on account of the performance of official duties relating to, or in support of recovery from, the presidentially-declared disaster or emergency, or any person assisting such an officer or employee in the performance of such duties, or on account of that assistance; or (2) forcibly assaults, resists, opposes, impedes, intimidates, or interferes with any person providing

services in support of disaster relief efforts and working in coordination with a federal coordinating officer appointed pursuant to section 302, Public Law 98-288 (42 U.S.C. 5143, shall except in subsection(b) of this section, be fined under this title or imprisoned not more than 2 years, or both. "(b) Whoever, in the commission of and in relation to any act described in subsection(a) of this section, carries, possesses or uses a deadly or dangerous weapon or inflicts serious bodily injury, shall be fined under this title or imprisoned not more than 15 years or both, or, if the death of any person results, shall be punished by death or life imprisonment," proposed 18 U.S.C. 1370 (H.R. 3150; the wording of H.R. 880 is comparable).

[121] "Any person who travels in or causes another (including the intended victim) to travel in interstate or foreign commerce, or uses or causes another (including the intended victim) to use the mail or any facility of interstate or foreign commerce, with intent that 2 or more murders be committed in violation of the laws of any state or the United States, or who conspires to do so . . . (3) if death results, may be fined not more than $250,000 under this title, and shall be punished by death or imprisonment for any term of years or for life." proposed 18 U.S.C. 1123.

[122] "(a) Any person who, during or in relation to any drug trafficking crime, murders . . . any individual. . . shall be punished, in addition and consecutive to the punishment provided for the drug trafficking crime – (1) in the case of murder, by death or imprisonment for any term of years or for life, a fine under title 18, United States Code, or both. . . . (d) As used in this section. . . (2) the term 'drug trafficking crime' has the meaning given that term in section 924(c)(2) of title 18, United States Code [*i.e.,* any felony punishable under the Controlled Substances Act (21 U.S.C. 801 et seq.), the Controlled Substances Import and Export Act (21 U.S.C. 951 et seq.) or the Maritime Drug Law Enforcement Act (46 U.S.C. 70501 et seq.)]," proposed 21 U.S.C. 865. (H.R. 3150; the wording of H.R. 880 is comparable).

[123] "Any person who, in furtherance or in aid of a criminal street gang, murders. . . any individual . . . shall be punished, in addition and consecutive to the punishment provided for any other violation of this chapter – (1) for murder, by death or imprisonment for any term of years or for life, a fine under this title, or both," proposed 18 U.S.C. 523.

[124] Proposed 18 U.S.C. 2339E(a).

[125] In a later section of H.R. 855, the bill amends 18 U.S.C. 2339A to make it punishable by imprisonment for not less than 30 years or for life, if death results from the commission of the offense. A court might conclude that amended section 2339A was intended to create an exception to the

application of section 2339E; *i.e.*, section 2339E applies to all federal crimes of terrorism other than 2339A.

[126] Proposed 18 U.S.C. 1952(d)(2).

[127] Proposed 18 U.S.C. 3281.

In: Capital Punishment Update
Editor: Lorraine V. Coyne, pp. 49-73
ISBN: 978-1-60456-133-3

Chapter 2

Capital Punishment: An Overview of Federal Death Penalty Statutes*

Elizabeth B. Bazan

Abstract

With the passage of P.L. 103-322, the Violent Crime Control and Law Enforcement Act of 1994, the federal death penalty became available as a possible punishment for a substantial number of new and existing civilian offenses. On April 24, 1996, the Antiterrorism and Effective Death Penalty Act of 1996 made further modifications and additions to the list of federal capital crimes. On June 25, 2002, P.L. 107-197, the Terrorist Bombings Convention Implementation Act of 2002, added another capital crime to the United States Code. The Intelligence Reform and Terrorism Prevention Act of 2004, P.L. 108-458, enacted December 17, 2004, included provisions which impacted or expanded some of the existing death penalty provisions. This article lists the current federal capital offenses and summarizes the procedures for federal civilian death penalty cases.

Introduction

With the passage of P.L. 103-322, the Violent Crime Control and Law Enforcement Act of 1994, the federal death penalty became available as a possible

* Excerpted from CRS Report RL30962, dated January 5, 2005.

punishment for a substantial number of new and existing civilian offenses. Further changes to the list of federal capital punishment statutes resulted from the passage of the Antiterrorism and Effective Death Penalty Act of 1996, P.L. 104-132, on April 24, 1996. On June 25, 2002, the Terrorist Bombings Convention Implementation Act of 2002, P.L. 107-197, added another capital crime to the United States Code. Some of the existing death penalty provisions were expanded, directly or indirectly, by the enactment on December 17, 2004, of the Intelligence Reform and Terrorism Prevention Act of 2004, P.L. 108-458. This article lists the current federal death penalty offenses and summarizes the procedures for civilian death penalty cases.[1]

CAPITAL OFFENSES

In *Furman v. Georgia,* 408 U.S. 238 (1972), the Supreme Court held unconstitutional a capital sentencing scheme which gave the sentencing decision-maker unbridled discretion in determining whether to impose a death sentence in a given case. Prior to the passage of the Violent Crime Control and Law Enforcement Act of 1994, P.L. 103-322, all but two[2] of the existing federal civilian death penalty provisions suffered from constitutional frailties like those of the Georgia statute at issue in *Furman*. The Act revived the death penalty for several previously unenforceable capital offenses, added capital punishment to the penalties available for a few other existing federal offenses and created a number of new capital offenses. The Antiterrorism and Effective Death Penalty Act of 1996, P.L. 104-132, expanded and modified the list of federal capital punishment offenses. Two other statutes further expanded the reach of the federal death penalty, the Terrorist Bombings Convention Implementation Act of 2002, P.L. 107-197, and the Intelligence Reform and Terrorism Prevention Act of 2004, P.L. 108-458. In the wake of these Acts, the death penalty is an available sentencing option for the following offenses:

- 7 U.S.C. § 2146(b)–first degree murder of any person while engaged in or on account of the performance of his or her official duties with respect to the transportation, sale, or handling of certain animals under 7 U.S.C. ch. 54, §§ 2131 *et seq*. This provision cross-references 18 U.S.C. §§ 1111 (murder) and 1114 (protection of officers and employees of the United States) for applicable punishment.
- 8 U.S.C. § 1324(a)–murder, with death resulting from smuggling aliens into the United States.

- 15 U.S.C. § 1825(a)(2)(C)–killing of an official while engaged in or on account of performance of his or her official duties under 15 U.S.C. § 1821 *et seq.*, which deals with protection of horses in horse shows, exhibitions, sales, or auctions.
- 18 U.S.C. §§ 32 and 34–willful destruction of aircraft within the special aircraft jurisdiction of the United States; of any civil aircraft used, operated, or employed in interstate, overseas or foreign air commerce; or of aircraft facilities, where death results.[3] Sections 32 and 34 also cover performing an act of violence or incapacitation against any individual on such aircraft which is likely to endanger the safety of the aircraft, where death results. Where a U.S. national is on board the civil aircraft involved or would have been on board, where an offender is a U.S. national, or where an offender is found in the U.S. after commission of such an offense, these provisions would also cover: engaging in a willful act of violence against an individual while on board a civil aircraft registered in a country other than the United States, which act is likely to endanger the aircraft in flight, where death results; willfully destroying a civil aircraft registered in a country other than the U.S. or damaging it so as to make it incapable of flight or endangering its safety in flight, where death results; or willfully placing a device or substance on such an aircraft likely to destroy that aircraft, to render it incapable of flight, or to endanger its safety while in flight, where death results.
- 18 U.S.C. §§ 33 and 34–willful destruction of motor vehicles engaged in interstate or foreign commerce, or their facilities, where death results.[4]
- 18 U.S.C. § 36–murder committed in furtherance of or to escape detection of a major drug offense by firing a weapon into a group of two or more people (drive-by shooting).[5]
- 18 U.S.C. § 37–murder, with death resulting from a violation of the proscription against the use of violence at international airports. U.S. jurisdiction under this provision covers instances where the prohibited activity takes place in the United States or where it takes place outside the United States and the offender is later found in the United States, or where an offender or a victim is a U.S. national. It does not cover instances where the relevant conduct was committed in the United States during or in connection with a labor dispute and the conduct is a felony under pertinent State law.[6]
- 18 U.S.C. § 115(b)(3)–first degree murder of a member of the immediate family of a United States official, a United States judge, a Federal law enforcement officer, or an official whose killing would be a crime under

18 U.S.C. § 1114, with intent to impede, intimidate, or interfere with such official, judge, or law enforcement officer while engaged in the performance of official duties, or with intent to retaliate against such official, judge, or law enforcement officer on account of the performance of official duties.

- 18 U.S.C. §§ 229 and 229A(a)(2)–knowingly developing, producing, acquiring, transferring directly or indirectly, receiving, stockpiling, retaining, owning, possessing, using, or threatening to use any chemical weapon; or knowingly assisting or inducing any person to do any of the above; or knowingly attempting or conspiring to do any of the above, where death results. The offenses are defined in 18 U.S.C. § 229 and do not cover retention, ownership, possession, transfer, or receipt of a chemical weapon by a department, agency, or other entity of the United States, pending destruction of the weapon. Also exempt from coverage of these offenses are persons, including members of the U.S. Armed Forces, authorized by law or by an appropriate officer of the United States to retain, own, possess, transfer or receive the chemical weapon pending destruction of the weapon. Similarly exempt is any otherwise nonculpable person, in an emergency situation, if the person is attempting to destroy or seize the weapon. This covers conduct committed within the United States; committed by a U.S. national outside the United States; committed against a U.S. national while the national is outside the United States; or committed against property owned, leased, or used by the United States or any federal agency or department, whether within or outside the United States.
- 18 U.S.C. § 241–murder, with death resulting from a conspiracy to violate civil rights. Also appears to provide for possible capital punishment where acts constituting a conspiracy against rights under this section involve kidnapping or attempted kidnapping, aggravated sexual abuse or attempted aggravated sexual abuse, or attempted killing, regardless of whether death results from the commission of the offense. *But see*, 18 U.S.C. § 3591(a)(2).[7]
- 18 U.S.C. § 242–murder, with death resulting from a deprivation of civil rights under color of law. Also appears to make capital punishment available for acts constituting a deprivation of rights under color of law involving kidnapping or attempted kidnapping, aggravated sexual abuse or attempted aggravated sexual abuse, or attempted killing, regardless of whether a death occurs during the commission of the offense. *But see*, 18 U.S.C. § 3591(a)(2).[8]

- 18 U.S.C. § 245(b)–murder, with death resulting from a deprivation of federally protected rights. Also appears to make death penalty available for deprivation of federally protected rights if such acts include kidnapping or an attempt to kidnap, aggravated sexual abuse or attempted aggravated sexual abuse, or attempted killing, regardless of whether a death occurs during the commission of the offense. *But see*, 18 U.S.C. § 3591(a)(2).[9]
- 18 U.S.C. § 247–murder, with death resulting from intentionally damaging religious property or intentionally obstructing the free exercise of religion. Also appears to make capital punishment available for acts which constitute intentionally damaging religious property or intentionally obstructing free exercise of religion involving kidnapping or attempted kidnapping, aggravated sexual abuse or attempted aggravated sexual abuse, or attempted killing. *But see*, 18 U.S.C. § 3591(a)(2).[10]
- 18 U.S.C. § 351–assassination of Members of Congress, the Cabinet, or the Supreme Court, or major Presidential or Vice Presidential candidates.
- 18 U.S.C. § 794(a), 18 U.S.C. § 3591(a)(1)–espionage resulting in the identification and consequent death of an agent of the United States, or involving nuclear weaponry, military spacecraft or satellites, early warning systems or other means of defense or retaliation against large-scale attack, war plans, communications intelligence or cryptographic information, or any other major weapons system or major element of defense strategy.[11]
- 18 U.S.C. § 794(b), 18 U.S.C. § 3591(a)(1)–espionage in time of war with intent that information be communicated to the enemy. Covers collection, recording, publishing, or communicating, or attempting to elicit any information with respect to movement, numbers, description, condition, or disposition of Armed Forces, ships, aircraft, or war materials of the United States; plans, conduct, or supposed plans or conduct of naval or military operations; any works or measures undertaken to fortify or defend any place; or any other information relating to the public defense, which might be useful to the enemy.[12]
- 18 U.S.C. § 844(d)–interstate transportation or receipt of explosives with the knowledge or intent that they are to be used to kill another, where death results directly or proximately to any person, "including any public safety officer performing duties."
- 18 U.S.C. § 844(f)(3)–malicious damage or destruction or attempted damage or destruction of any building, vehicle, or other personal or real property in whole or in part owned or possessed by, or leased to, the

United States or any department or agency thereof through use of fire or explosives, where the conduct directly or proximately caused the death of any person, "including any public safety officer performing duties."

- 18 U.S.C. § 844(i)–malicious damage or destruction or attempted damage or destruction, through the use of fire or explosives, of real or personal property used in interstate or foreign commerce or used in any activity affecting such commerce, where death results directly or proximately to any person, "including any public safety officer performing duties."
- 18 U.S.C. § 924(c) and (j)(1)–gun murders during federal crimes of violence or drug trafficking crimes.
- 18 U.S.C. § 930–first degree murder involving use of firearm or other dangerous weapon during attack on a federal facility.
- 18 U.S.C. § 1091–genocide committed in the United States or by a United States national.
- 18 U.S.C. § 1111–first degree murder within the special maritime or territorial jurisdiction of the United States.[13]
- 18 U.S.C. § 1114–first degree murder of federal officers or employees, including members of the uniformed services, while such officer or employee is engaged in or on account of the performance of official duties, or of any person assisting such officer or employee in the performance of such duties or on account of that assistance.
- 18 U.S.C. § 1116(a)–first degree murder of foreign officials, official guests, or internationally protected persons. Authorizes United States jurisdiction over the offense if the victim is an internationally protected person outside the United States where the victim is a representative, officer, employee, or agent of the United States; where an offender is a U.S. national; or where an offender is afterwards found in the United States.
- 18 U.S.C. § 1118–murder by a federal prisoner serving life sentence at the time of the offense.
- 18 U.S.C. § 1119–first degree murder of U.S. national outside the United States but within the jurisdiction of a foreign country.
- 18 U.S.C. § 1120–first degree murder by escaped federal prisoner who was confined under a life sentence.
- 18 U.S.C. § 1121–murder of state or local official, officer, or employee, or other person aiding federal criminal investigations, or of state correctional officer while the victim is engaged in the performance of official duties, because of the performance of such duties, or because of the victim's status as a public servant.

- 18 U.S.C. § 1201–violation of federal kidnapping laws where death results. Except in the case of kidnapping of a minor by his or her parent, this section covers kidnapping when the victim is transported in interstate or foreign commerce; when the act is committed within the special maritime or territorial jurisdiction of the United States or within the special aircraft jurisdiction of the United States; when the victim is a foreign official, internationally protected person, or official guest; or when the victim is a federal officer or employee covered by 18 U.S.C. § 1114 who is kidnapped while engaged in or on account of performance of official duties. Where the victim is an internationally protected person outside the United States, U.S. jurisdiction is authorized if the victim is a representative, officer, employee, or agent of the United States; if an offender is a U.S. national; or if an offender is afterwards found in the United States.
- 18 U.S.C. § 1203–hostage taking where death results.
- 18 U.S.C. § 1503–first degree murder of court officer or juror in federal judicial proceedings.
- 18 U.S.C. § 1512–murder, with death resulting from tampering with a federal witness, victim or informant.
- 18 U.S.C. § 1513–first degree murder, with death resulting from retaliation against a federal witness, victim or informant.
- 18 U.S.C. § 1716–mailing or depositing for mailing nonmailable injurious articles where death results.
- 18 U.S.C. § 1751(a), (b)–assassination/first degree murder of the President; President-elect; Vice President; or, if there is no Vice President, the officer next in order of succession to the Presidency; of the Vice President-elect; of another person acting as President under the Constitution and laws of the United States; or of certain employees of the Executive Office of the President or of the Office of the Vice President. Also covers kidnapping of any of these officials or employees, where death results.
- 18 U.S.C. § 1958–murder, with death resulting from the use of facilities of interstate commerce in the commission of a murder for hire.
- 18 U.S.C. § 1959(a)(1)–murder, as consideration for receipt of, or as consideration for a promise or agreement to pay, anything of pecuniary value from an enterprise engaged in racketeering activity; or murder for the purpose of gaining entrance to or maintaining or increasing position in an enterprise engaged in racketeering activity.[14]

- 18 U.S.C. § 1992–murder, with death resulting from wrecking trains or related structures, facilities or appurtenances, employed in interstate commerce.
- 18 U.S.C. § 2113(e)–murder, with the death resulting from: robbery or attempted robbery of a federally insured bank or savings and loan association or credit union; knowing receipt of stolen goods from such a robbery; avoiding or attempting to avoid apprehension for such an offense; or escaping or attempting to escape from arrest or confinement from such an offense.
- 18 U.S.C. § 2119(3)–murder, with death resulting from carjacking or attempted carjacking, of a car transported in interstate commerce.
- 18 U.S.C. § 2245–murder, with death resulting from a federal sexual abuse offense.[15]
- 18 U.S.C. § 2251–murder, with death resulting from violation of federal laws against sexual exploitation of children.
- 18 U.S.C. § 2280–violence against maritime navigation where death results: committed against or on board a ship flying the United States flag; committed in the United States where the activity is not prohibited by pertinent state criminal law; committed by a United States national or a stateless person who habitually resides in the United States; committed against a United States national; committed to coerce the United States; or committed by one later found within the United States.
- 18 U.S.C. § 2281–murder, with death resulting from violence committed aboard a fixed ocean platform within the United States or by a United States national or against a United States national, committed to coerce the United States, or committed by one later found within the United States.
- 18 U.S.C. § 2332(a)(1)–murder of a United States national overseas.
- 18 U.S.C. § 2332a–where death results, use, attempted use, or conspiracy to use, weapons of mass destruction (1) against a United States national outside the United States; (2) against any person or property within the United States, where either (A) the mail or any facility of interstate or foreign commerce is used in furtherance of the offense, (B) such property is used in interstate or foreign commerce or in an activity that affects interstate or foreign commerce, (C) any perpetrator travels in or causes another to travel in interstate or foreign commerce in furtherance of the offense, or (D) the offense or the results of the offense affect interstate or foreign commerce or, in the case of a threat, attempt or conspiracy, would have affected interstate or foreign commerce;[16] (3) against any property

owned, leased or used by the federal government; or (4) against any property within the United States that is owned, leased, or used by a foreign government. 18 U.S.C. § 2332a(a). Subsection 2332a(b), added by P.L. 104-132 and amended by P.L. 108-458, makes the death penalty also available with respect to any U.S. national who, without lawful authority, uses or threatens, attempts, or conspires to use a weapon of mass destruction outside of the United States, where death results. P.L. 104-132 modified the definition of "weapon of mass destruction," to include any destructive device as defined in 18 U.S.C. § 921; any weapon that is designed or intended to cause death or serious bodily injury through the release, dissemination, or impact of toxic or poisonous chemicals, or their precursors; any weapon involving a disease organism; or any weapon that is designed to release radiation or radioactivity at a level dangerous to human life. However, before passage of Section 6802(b) of P.L. 108-458, both 18 U.S.C. §§ 2332a(a) and (b) excluded chemical weapons as defined under 18 U.S.C. § 229F from the "weapons of mass destruction" included in the elements of these offenses. Section 6802(b) eliminated that exclusion so that the offenses defined in 18 U.S.C. §§ 2332a(a) and (b) now can involve such chemical weapons.[17]

- 18 U.S.C. § 2332b–acts of terrorism transcending national boundaries, where death results. Specifically prohibits killing, kidnapping, maiming, committing an assault resulting in serious bodily injury or committing an assault with a dangerous weapon within the United States. Also prohibits creating a substantial risk of serious bodily injury to another by destroying or damaging any structure, conveyance, or other real or personal property within the United States, or attempting or conspiring to do so, where the conduct transcends national boundaries and meets set jurisdictional criteria. Those criteria include: the offender used the mails or any facility of interstate or foreign commerce; the offense obstructed, delayed or affected interstate or foreign commerce, or the offense would have done so if consummated; the victim or intended victim is the U.S. government, a member of the uniformed services, or any official, officer, employee, or agent of the any of the three branches of the U.S. government or of any department or agency of the United States; the structure, conveyance or other real or personal property is, in whole or in part, owned, possessed, or leased by the United States or a department or agency thereof; the offense is committed in the territorial sea of the United States, including the airspace above, the seabed and subsoil below, and artificial islands and fixed structures erected thereon; or the offense is committed within the special maritime or territorial jurisdiction of the United States. The death penalty is available for any such offense involving a killing or resulting in death to any person from conduct prohibited by this section.

- 18 U.S.C. § 2332f–unlawfully delivering, placing, discharging, or detonating an explosive or other lethal device in, into, or against a place of public use, a government facility, a public transportation system, or an infrastructure facilities, with intent to cause death or serious bodily injury or to cause extensive destruction, where such destruction causes or is likely to cause major economic loss, where death results.[18]
- 18 U.S.C. § 2340A–torture or attempted torture committed outside the United States by a person acting under color of law, where death results. United States jurisdiction under this provision covers offenses where the alleged offender is a U.S. national or where the alleged offender is present in the United States, regardless of the nationality of the victim or alleged offender.
- 18 U.S.C. § 2381, 18 U.S.C. § 2391(a)(1); U.S. Constitution, Article 3, Sec. 3, cl. 1–treason by a person owing allegiance to the United States. Involves either levying war against the United States or adhering to enemies of the United States, giving aid and comfort to them either within the United States or elsewhere. Constitution provides that no person shall be convicted of treason except on the testimony of two witnesses to the same overt act or on confession in open court.[19]
- 18 U.S.C. § 2441–War crimes committed by or against a member of the Armed Forces of the United States or a national of the United States as defined in section 101 of the Immigration and Nationality Act, 8 U.S.C. § 1101,[20] where death results.
- 21 U.S.C. § 461–killing of a person engaged in or on account of his or her official duties under 21 U.S.C. § 451 *et seq.*, with respect to inspection of poultry or poultry products.
- 21 U.S.C. § 675–killing of a person engaged in or on account of his or her official duties with respect to meat inspection under 21 U.S.C. § 601 *et seq.*
- 21 U.S.C. § 848(c)(1), 18 U.S.C. § 3591(b)(1)–drug kingpin violation committed as part of a continuing enterprise under conditions set forth in 21 U.S.C. § 848(b), involving twice the amount of controlled substances specified in 21 U.S.C. § 848(b)(2)(A) or twice the gross receipts specified in 21 U.S.C. § 848(b)(2)(B).[21]

- 21 U.S.C. § 848(c)(1), 18 U.S.C. § 3591(b)(2)–attempted murder by a drug kingpin endeavoring to obstruct justice.[22]
- 21 U.S.C. § 848(e)(1)–intentional killing in the course of a violation of the drug kingpin statute.
- 21 U.S.C. § 848(e)(1)–murder of a law enforcement officer in furtherance of a controlled substances offense.
- 21 U.S.C. § 1041–killing of a person engaged in or on account of his or her official duties under 21 U.S.C. § 1031 *et seq.*, with respect to inspection of eggs and egg products.
- 49 U.S.C. §§ 46502(a)(2)(B) and (b)(1)(B)–air piracy, where death of another person results from the commission or the attempt. Subsection 46502(a)(2)(B) applies to aircraft piracy committed within the special aircraft jurisdiction of the United States. Subsection 46502(b)(1)(B) applies to an offense committed on an aircraft in flight outside the special aircraft jurisdiction of the United States and later found in the United States, where the takeoff or landing of the aircraft involved was located outside the territory of the aircraft's country of registration.

Capital Sentencing Procedures

Under 18 U.S.C. § 3432, a capital defendant must be provided a copy of the indictment and a list of veniremen and prosecution witnesses, stating the place of abode of each, at least three full days before trial begins. P.L. 103-322 amended this provision to permit the list of veniremen and witnesses to be withheld from a capital defendant if the court finds by a preponderance of the evidence that providing the list may jeopardize the life or safety of any person.

P.L. 103-322 also amended 18 U.S.C. § 3005 to provide that the trial court in a capital case shall, upon defendant's request, promptly assign two counsel, at least one of whom shall be learned in the law applicable to capital cases. Counsel shall have free access to the accused at all reasonable hours. In assigning such counsel, the court must consider the recommendations of the Federal Public Defender organization, if one exists in the district. Otherwise, the recommendation of the Administrative Office of the United States Courts must be taken into account.

Sentencing procedures for federal civilian capital cases are codified at 18 U.S.C. §§ 3591-3598.[23] The government must give a capital defendant timely notice before trial or before a guilty plea is accepted that the prosecution intends to seek a death sentence and must specify the aggravating factor or factors upon which it intends to rely for this purpose.[24] This notice must be filed with the court.[25] The new statutory procedures specify mitigating and aggravating factors to be considered in determining whether a death sentence is warranted in a given case.[26] In addition to the specified mitigating factors,[27] other factors in the defendant's background, record, or character or any other mitigating circumstances may be considered. In addition to the specified aggravating factors,[28] the jury, or if there is no jury, the court, may consider whether any other aggravating factor for which notice has been given exists.[29]

In a capital case, a separate sentencing hearing must be held before a jury or, if there is no jury, before the court.[30] The government must prove aggravating factors beyond a reasonable doubt, while the defendant must prove mitigating factors by a preponderance of the information.[31] Where the hearing is before a jury, aggravating factors must be found unanimously. Special findings as to mitigating factors may be made by one or more members of the jury.[32] If no aggravating factors are found, the court must impose a sentence other than death.[33]

The jury must be instructed that its capital sentencing decision must not involve any consideration of the race, color, religious beliefs, national origin, or gender of the defendant or of any victim. Each juror must certify that these considerations were not involved in his or her individual decision and that the juror would have made the same sentencing recommendation regardless of the race, color, religious beliefs, national origin, or sex of the defendant or of any victim.[34]

No one may be sentenced to death for an offense committed while under the age of 18.[35] Nor can a death sentence be carried out upon a pregnant woman,[36] a person who is mentally retarded, or who, because of a mental disability, lacks the capacity to understand the death penalty and the reason it was imposed.[37] Finally, a death penalty may not be imposed under these death penalty provisions upon a person subject to the criminal jurisdiction of an Indian tribal government for an offense which occurred within Indian country and for which federal jurisdiction is based "solely upon Indian country," unless the tribe's governing body has elected to have the new capital sentencing procedures in 18 U.S.C. ch. 228, §§ 3591-3598, applicable to the land and persons subject to its criminal jurisdiction.[38]

The law provides for mandatory review of a death sentence upon timely notice filed. The court of appeals will reverse and remand for resentencing upon a finding that the sentence was the product of prejudice or passion, that the evidence does not support the finding of the existence of an aggravating factor, or that legal error requiring reversal exists.[39]

Once appeals are exhausted, an execution is to be conducted according to the laws of the state in which the sentence is imposed. If the laws of that state do not provide for implementation of a death sentence, the court will designate another state which does have such laws, and the execution will be carried out in the manner prescribed by the latter state's laws.[40] State or local facilities may be used for execution. The United States marshal charged with supervising the implementation of the death sentence may also use the services of state or local officials or of a person such officials employ for that purpose. However, neither federal nor state employees may be required to participate in a capital prosecution or execution.[41]

REFERENCES

[1] While a discussion of the death penalty provisions applicable to military personnel is beyond the scope of this paper, there are a number of these statutory provisions in the Uniform Code of Military Justice, including: 10 U.S.C. §§ 885 (desertion in time of war); 890 (assaulting or willfully disobeying a superior commissioned officer in time of war); 894 (mutiny, sedition, attempted mutiny, or failure to suppress or report a mutiny or sedition); 899 (misbehavior before the enemy); 900 (subordinate compelling surrender); 901 (improper use of countersign in time of war); 902 (forcing a safeguard); 904 (aiding the enemy); 906 (spying in time of war); 910 (improper hazarding of a vessel); 913 (misbehavior of a sentinel in time of war); and 918 (premeditated murder or murder in the course of burglary, sodomy, rape, robbery, or aggravated arson). A military death penalty statute creating a capital offense for the commission of espionage in violation of the Uniform Code of Military Justice, enacted in the 99th Congress, is codified at 10 U.S.C. § 906a. The sentencing procedures set forth for the court-martial in this section specify aggravating and mitigating factors to be considered, require special findings regarding the existence of these factors, and direct that an accused may have broad latitude in presenting mitigating or extenuating evidence. This statute evidently was intended to conform to minimum constitutional standards, but the Supreme Court has not yet passed upon its constitutional validity. 10 U.S.C. § 920(a) also provides for capital punishment as a possible punishment for rape. Under Rule 1004(c)(9) of the Rules for Court-Martial in the *Manual for Courts-Martial*, the death penalty is only available as a sentencing option in a rape case under 10 U.S.C. § 920 if "(A) The victim was under the age of

12; or (B) The accused maimed or attempted to kill the victim." In Coker v. Georgia, 433 U.S. 584 (1984), the United States Supreme Court held the death penalty disproportionate, under the Eighth Amendment's prohibition of cruel and unusual punishment, to the rape of an adult woman by an escaped felon who had been serving sentences for murder, rape, kidnapping, and aggravated assault at the time of his escape, where the victim survived. (For more discussion of the *Coker* decision, see fn. 7, *infra.*) In United States v. Matthews, 16 M.J. 354 (C.M.A. 1983), *on remand,* 17 M.J. 978 (C.M.R. 1984) (substituting confinement for life at hard labor for death penalty), *review denied,* 18 M.J. 401 (C.M.A. 1984), the United States Court of Military Appeals observed that: Congress obviously intended that in cases where an accused service member is convicted of premeditated murder, certain types of felony murder, or rape, the court-martial members should have the option to adjudge a death sentence. See Articles 118 and 120 [10 U.S.C. § 918 and 920]. Probably this intent cannot be constitutionally effectuated in a case where the rape of an adult female is involved, Coker v. Georgia, 433 U.S. 584 . . . (1977) – at least, where there is no purpose unique to the military mission that would be served by allowing the death penalty for this offense. . . .16 M.J. at 380. *See,* United States v. Rojas, 15 M.J. 902, 927 n. 9 (N.M.C.M.R. 1983, *remanded on other grounds*, 17 M.J. 154 (C.M.A. 1984); United States v. Clark, 18 M.J. 775, 776 (N.M.C.M.R. 1984) ("Current appellate decisional authority indicates that the offense of rape, as alleged against the appellant, is not an offense for which the death penalty can be adjudged. . . . A sentence of death for the crime of rape of an adult woman is prohibited by the Eighth Amendment to the U.S. Constitution. Coker v. Georgia, 433 U.S. 584, . . . (1977). Therefore, the capital aspect of punishment purportedly authorized under Article 120 has been effectively invalidated."); United States v. Christie, 1995 CCA LEXIS 220 (A.F. Ct. Crim. App. August 28, 1995); United States v. Clark, 18 M.J. 775, 776 (N-M. Ct. Crim. App. 1984); United States v. McReynolds, 9 M.J. 881, 882 (A.F.C.M.R. 1980). *See also,* United States v. Curtis, 32 M.J. 252, 266 (C.M.A. 1991), and United States v. Straight, 42 M.J. 244, 247 (C.A.A.F 1995), interpreting Rule 1004(c)(9) as having been drafted in an effort to comply with *Coker.* Prior to enactment of 10 U.S.C. § 906a, President Reagan issued an executive order which changed the sentencing procedures in the Manual of Courts-Martial in an apparent attempt to conform them to minimum constitutional standards. E.O. 12473, issued April 13, 1984. In Loving v. United States, 517 U.S.748 (1996), *writ of mandamus denied,* 47 M.J. 438 (C.A.A.F. 1998), *cert.*

denied, 525 U.S. 1040 (1998), the Supreme Court addressed a constitutional challenge on Eighth Amendment and separation of powers grounds to the aggravating factors applicable to military death penalty cases promulgated by executive order and included in Rule for Courts-Martial (RCM) 1004, as amended. Loving contended that fundamental policy determinations with respect to aggravating factors in death penalty cases must be made by Congress through statutory enactments, rather than by the President. The Court, assuming that Furman v. Georgia, 408 U.S. 238 (1972), and subsequent cases applied to the crime and sentence before it, found that the aggravating factors included in RCM 1004 were necessary, from a constitutional perspective, to adequately narrow the class of persons eligible to receive the death penalty under the statute under which Loving was convicted and sentenced. Further, the Court rejected Loving's contention that the President's promulgation of these aggravating factors by executive order violated separation of powers principles. The Court found that the Congress had the power to delegate the authority to prescribe aggravating factors in military capital murder cases to the President, and had in fact made a valid delegation of that authority in 10 U.S.C. §§ 818, 836(a) and 856. The Court also found a connection between the delegated authority and the President's constitutional duties as Commander in Chief. The capital sentencing procedures governing civilian capital cases first added by P.L. 103-322, Title VI, Sec. 60002(a), codified at 18 U.S.C. §§ 3591-3598, as amended, do not apply to "prosecutions under the Uniform Code of Military Justice (10 U.S.C. § 801)." P.L. 103-322, Title VI, Sec. 60004, 18 U.S.C. § 3591 note.

[2] In 1974, the Congress enacted a death penalty statute for air piracy where death resulted from the commission of the offense, and responded to the concerns reflected in *Furman* by including procedures designed to tailor the sentencing discretion of the judge or jury in determining the appropriate sentence to impose in the case before them. The substantive provisions were codified at 49 U.S.C. §§ 1472(i) and (n) (49 U.S.C. § 46502 in the revised Title 49 of the United States Code), while the procedures for a separate sentencing hearing, specifying aggravating and mitigating factors to be considered in the sentencing determination, and requiring a special verdict finding the existence or non-existence of each of the factors, were codified at then existing 49 U.S.C. App. § 1473(c)/49 U.S.C. § 46503. The constitutional sufficiency of these procedures was not tested. They might have given rise to a question as to whether they satisfied the constitutional minimum in light of the Supreme Court's decision in Lockett v. Ohio, 438

U.S. 586, 604 (1978), which held invalid Ohio's death penalty statute because it failed to permit consideration, in a capital case, of any aspects of the defendant's character or record or the circumstances of the offense as a mitigating factor. The federal air piracy sentencing provisions in former 49 U.S.C. App. § 1473(c)/49 U.S.C. § 46503 appeared to limit the mitigating factors which may be considered in a capital case, and therefore might have been subject to attack. The death penalty sentencing procedures for aircraft piracy in former 49 U.S.C. App. 1473(c)/49 U.S.C. § 46503 were repealed by Sec. 60003(b)(2), 108 Stat. 1970, of P.L. 103-322. In a capital aircraft piracy case under current law, the general death penalty sentencing provisions in 18 U.S.C. § 3591 *et seq.* would apply. For a discussion of capital sentencing provisions, see the discussion of capital sentencing procedures starting at page 13, *infra.* In the Anti-Drug Abuse Act of 1988, P.L. 100-690, the death penalty was made available for certain controlled substances offenses where intentional death resulted from the offense. 21 U.S.C. §§ 848(e) and (g)-(r). The measure, as amended, includes sentencing procedures which provide for a separate sentencing hearing; specifies aggravating and mitigating factors, detailing the means of proof and requiring special findings concerning them; and supplies instruction for the imposition, appeal, and execution of a death sentence. The availability of counsel as well as investigative, expert and other services for indigent defendants is also addressed. The composition of the jury is specified, and the jury is required to return to the court a certificate signed by each juror indicating that discrimination played no part in his or her sentencing decision. Thus far, these capital sentencing provisions have withstood constitutional challenge.

[3] The offense is set forth generally in 18 U.S.C. § 32, while the penalty for commission of the offense where death results is drawn from 18 U.S.C. § 34. The latter section makes the death penalty available for offenses prohibited by 18 U.S.C. ch. 2 (§§ 31-38), which result in the death of any person.

[4] The offense is set forth generally in 18 U.S.C. § 33, while the penalty for commission of the offense where death results is specified in 18 U.S.C. § 34.

[5] *See also*, 18 U.S.C. § 34, which makes capital punishment available for any offense prohibited by 18 U.S.C. ch. 2 (§§ 31-38) where death results.

[6] *See also*, 18 U.S.C. § 34, which makes the death penalty available for any offense prohibited by 18 U.S.C. ch. 2 (§§ 31-38) where death results.

[7] Under the Supreme Court's reasoning in Coker v. Georgia, 433 U.S. 584 (1977), and its progeny, a death penalty imposed under such circumstances, where the commission of the offense did not result in a death, might give rise to a question as to whether the punishment imposed was disproportionate to the crime committed. *Coker* involved the rape of an adult woman by an escaped felon who had been serving sentences for murder, rape, kidnapping, and aggravated assault at the time of his escape, where the victim survived. The Court, while acknowledging the seriousness of the crime, found the death penalty disproportionate to the offense. This case has given rise to questions as to whether the death penalty would be found appropriate, under Eighth Amendment cruel and unusual standards, for any offense where a death did not result. *See, e.g., Coker*, 433 U.S., at 621 (Burger, C.J., dissenting). Indeed, Chief Justice Burger also raised a question as to whether the death penalty might also be open to challenge under the plurality's reasoning for crimes such as "treason," "airplane hijacking, kidnapping, and mass terrorist activity," which, although dangerous and constituting a serious threat to public safety, did not necessarily result in immediate death. *Id.* Similar reasoning might give rise to a question as to the constitutionality of a death penalty for espionage where death did not result from the commission of the offense. Except with respect to espionage and treason as addressed in 18 U.S.C. § 3591(a)(1), and certain controlled substances offenses referred to in 18 U.S.C. § 3591(b), the *Coker* issue raised by provision of a death penalty for offenses not involving death may be minimized by the impact of 18 U.S.C. § 3591(a)(2), which provides that a death sentence may be imposed upon a defendant found guilty of (2) any other offense for which a sentence of death is provided, if the defendant, as determined beyond a reasonable doubt at the hearing under section 3593--(A) intentionally killed the victim; (B) intentionally inflicted serious bodily injury that resulted in the death of the victim; (C) intentionally participated in an act, contemplating that the life of a person would be taken or intending that lethal force would be used in connection with a person other than one of the participants in the offense, and the victim died as a direct result of that act; or (D) intentionally and specifically engaged in an act of violence, knowing that the act created a grave risk of death to a person, other than one of the participants in the offense, such that participation in the act constituted a reckless disregard for human life and the victim died as a direct result of the act, ... Under Subsection 3591(a)(1), the death penalty is made available in cases where the defendant has been found guilty of an offense described in 18 U.S.C. §

794 (espionage) or § 2381 (treason), without explicitly restricting the availability of capital punishment to those cases in which death results. Subsection 3591(b) makes the death penalty available for a defendant who has been found guilty of (1) an offense referred to in section 408(c)(1) of the Controlled Substances Act (21 U.S.C. 848(c)(1)), committed as part of a continuing criminal enterprise offense under the conditions described in subsection (b) of that section which involved not less than twice the quantity of controlled substance described in subsection (b)(2)(A) or twice the gross receipts described in subsection (b)(2)(B); or (2) an offense referred to in section 408(c)(1) of the Controlled Substances Act (21 U.S.C. 848(c)(1)), committed as part of a continuing criminal enterprise offense under that section, where the defendant is a principal administrator, organizer, or leader of such an enterprise, and the defendant, in order to obstruct the investigation or prosecution of the enterprise or an offense involved in the enterprise, attempts to kill or knowingly directs, advises, authorizes, or assists another to attempt to kill any public officer, juror, witness, or member of the family or household of such person, ...

[8] As discussed in greater depth at fn. 7, above, it is questionable whether the death penalty may be constitutionally applied in cases where the offense committed does not result in death, in light of the Supreme Court's 1977 decision in Coker v. Georgia, *supra.* Note that operation of 18 U.S.C. § 3591(a)(2) would appear to limit the availability of the death penalty where death did not result from commission of an offense under 18 U.S.C. § 242, despite language in the offense statute that appears to provide for possible capital punishment.

[9] It is questionable whether the death penalty can constitutionally be applied in cases where the offense does not result in death, in light of the Supreme Court's decision in Coker v. Georgia, *supra,* as discussed in greater depth at fn. 7, above. Note that operation of 18 U.S.C. § 3591(a)(2) would seem to limit the availability of the death penalty for offenses under 18 U.S.C. § 245(b) which do not result in death, even though the language of the offense provision appears to provide for possible capital punishment.

[10] As discussed in greater depth at fn. 7, *supra,* it is uncertain whether the death penalty may be applied to offenses which do not result in death in light of the Supreme Court's decision in Coker v. Georgia, *supra.* Note that operation of 18 U.S.C. § 3591(a)(2) would appear to limit the availability of the death penalty for offenses under 18 U.S.C. § 247 which do not result in death, even though the language of the offense provision appears to provide for possible capital punishment.

[11] It is uncertain whether the death penalty may be applied to offenses which do not result in death, in light of the Supreme Court's analysis in Coker v. Georgia, *supra*, which is discussed in greater depth at fn. 7, *supra*. The issue would be whether, under the Eighth Amendment's cruel and unusual standard, the penalty would be deemed disproportionate to the crime. *But see*, U.S. v. Regan, 221 F. Supp. 2d 661 (E.D. Va. 2002) (denying defendant's motion to strike government's Notice of Intention to Seek the Death Penalty in a case where the defendant was charged with attempted espionage and there was no allegation of death resulting from the commission of the offense. Defendant premised his motion not on *Coker*, but on an Eighth Amendment comparative proportionality argument. Statutory aggravating factors were that, in commission of the offense the defendant knowingly created a grave risk of substantial danger to the national security; and that, in commission of the offense the defendant knowingly created a grave risk of death to another person.).

[12] In light of the Court's reasoning in Coker v. Georgia, *supra*, as discussed at fn. 7, *supra*, a death sentence imposed for this offense may be subject to an Eighth Amendment challenge on the grounds that the punishment is disproportionate to the crime. Such a challenge would appear to have less force if the commission of the offense caused someone's death; such a result may be likely considering the nature of the information which may be involved in such war-time disclosures and the potential impact of such disclosures.

[13] 49 U.S.C. § 46506(1) extends federal criminal jurisdiction to certain offenses committed aboard an aircraft in flight. One of the offenses referenced by this subsection is 18 U.S.C. § 1111.

[14] Section 6802(e) of P.L. 108-458, the Intelligence Reform and Terrorism Prevention Act of 2004, expands the list of offenses considered "racketeering activity" as defined in 18 U.S.C. § 1961 to include any act which is indictable under 18 U.S.C. §§ 175-178 (relating to biological weapons), sections 229-229F (relating to chemical weapons), and section 831(relating to nuclear weapons). Under 18 U.S.C. § 1959(b), "racketeering activity" as used in § 1959 has the meaning set forth in § 1961, so the effect of the expansion of the definition of "racketeering activity" is, in part, to indirectly expand the possible circumstances in which the death penalty may be available under 18 U.S.C. § 1959.

[15] 49 U.S.C. § 46506(1) extends federal criminal jurisdiction to certain offenses committed aboard an aircraft in flight, including 18 U.S.C. ch.

109A, dealing with sexual abuse. Among the provisions of Chapter 109A is 18 U.S.C. § 2245, added by P.L. 103-322.

[16] Section 6802(a) of P.L. 108-458 amended subsection (2) of 18 U.S.C. §2332a(a), expanding the range of potential targets or victims covered by the offense. Section 6802(a) of P.L. 108-458 also added subsection (4), again broadening the range of factual situations covered by the offense. In addition, it amended 18 U.S.C. § 2332a(c) to add a new definition of "property,"including all real and personal property. Section 6802(b) of P.L. 108-458 expanded the scope of "weapons of mass destruction" covered by the offense provisions in both 18 U.S.C. §§ 2332a(a) and (b) to include chemical weapons as defined in 18 U.S.C. § 229F. By expanding the victims, targets, and circumstances covered by the offense provisions in 18 U.S.C. §§ 2332a(a) and (b), Section 6802 of P.L. 108-458 expanded the circumstances in which the death penalty might be available where death resulted from the commission of the offenses involved.

[17] 18 U.S.C. § 229F defines the term "chemical weapon to mean, together or separately: a toxic chemical and its precursors, except where intended for a purpose not prohibited under 18 U.S.C., chapter 11B, as long as the type and quantity is consistent with such a purpose; a munition or device, specifically designed to cause death or other harm through toxic properties of such toxic chemicals, which would be released as a result of the employment of such a munition or device; and/or any equipment specifically designed for use directly in connection with the employment of such munitions or devices.

[18] This provision was added on June 25, 2002, as part of the Terrorist Bombings Convention Implementation Act of 2002, P.L. 107-197, Section 102(a), 116 Stat. 721. For applicable criminal penalties, the section cross references to 18 U.S.C. § 2332c. Federal jurisdiction over the offenses in 18 U.S.C. § 2332f is based on the existence of the following specified circumstances: If the offense is committed in the United States, (1) the offense must be committed against another nation or political subdivision thereof or a governmental facility of such nation or political subdivision, including its embassy, other diplomatic or consular premises; (2) the offense must be committed in an attempt to compel another nation or political subdivision thereof or the United States to act or to abstain from acting; (3) the offense must be committed on board a vessel flying the flag of another nation, on board an aircraft registered under the laws of another nation, or on board an aircraft operated by the government of another nation or political subdivision thereof; (4) a perpetrator is found outside the United

States; (5) a perpetrator is a national of another nation or a stateless person; or (6) a victim is a national of another nation or a stateless person. If the offense takes place outside the United States, (1) a perpetrator must be a U.S. national; (2) a victim must be a U.S. national; (3) a perpetrator must be found in the United States; (4) the offense must be committed in an attempt to compel the U.S. to do or abstain from doing any act; (5) the offense must be committed against a governmental facility of the United States or a political subdivision thereof, including a U.S. embassy or other diplomatic or consular premises; (6) the offense must be committed on board a vessel flying the U.S. flag or registered under U.S. law at the time the offense was committed; or (7) the offense must be committed on board an aircraft operated by the United States. Federal jurisdiction does not apply to the activities of armed forces during an armed conflict under the laws of war; to activities undertaken by military forces of a state in exercise of their official duties; or to offenses committed within the United States, where both the alleged offender and the victim(s) are U.S. citizens and the alleged offender is found within the U.S.; or where jurisdiction is predicated solely on the nationality of the victims or the alleged offender and the offense has no substantial effect on interstate or foreign commerce.

[19] If no death results from the commission of this offense, then, under the reasoning of the Court in Coker v. Georgia, *supra*, a death sentence imposed for this crime may be open to constitutional challenge. See discussion in fn. 7, *supra*.

[20] 22 U.S.C. § 1101(a)(22) defines "national of the United States" to mean "(A) a citizen of the United States, or (B) a person who, though not a citizen of the United States, owes permanent allegiance to the United States."

[21] As noted in fn. 7, *supra*, it is questionable, in light of the Supreme Court's decision in Coker v. Georgia, *supra*, whether the death penalty may be constitutionally applied to cases where a death does not result from the commission of the offense.

[22] The imposition of a death sentence for this offense might also give rise to an Eighth Amendment proportionality challenge under Coker v. Georgia, *supra*, *see* fn. 7, *supra*.

[23] These capital sentencing procedures were added by P.L. 103-322, Title VI, Sept. 13, 1994, 108 Stat. 1960 ; and have been amended by P.L. 103-322 Title XXXIII, § 330021(1), Sept. 13, 1994, 108 Stat. 1960, 2150; P.L. 104-132, Title VII, § 728, April 13, 1996,110 Stat. 1302; P.L. 104-294, Title VI, §§ 601(b)(7), 604(b)(35), Oct. 11, 1996, 110 Stat. 3499, 3508; P.L. 105-6, §

2(c), March. 19, 1997, 111 Stat. 12; and P.L. 107-273, Div. B., Title IV, §§ 4002(e)(2) and 4002(e)(8), Nov. 2, 2002, 116 Stat. 1810.

[24] 18 U.S.C. § 3593(a).

[25] Id.

[26] 18 U.S.C. § 3592.

[27] Under 18 U.S.C. § 3592(a), specified mitigating factors may include: a defendant's impaired capacity; the fact that the defendant acted under unusual and substantial duress; the defendant's minor participation in the capital offense; the fact that equally culpable defendant(s) will not be punished by death; the fact that the defendant has no prior criminal record; the defendant's severe mental or emotional disturbance when committing the offense; and the victim's consent to the conduct which resulted in his or her death.

[28] 18 U.S.C. § 3592(b) sets out aggravating factors applicable to treason or espionage capital offenses, including a defendant's prior espionage or treason offense for which he or she could have been sentenced to life imprisonment or death, the fact that the defendant knowingly created a grave risk of substantial danger to national security in the commission of the offense at bar, or the fact that the defendant knowingly created a grave risk of death to another person in commission of the offense. 18 U.S.C. § 3592(c) sets forth sixteen aggravating factors for homicide. Among these are: the fact that the death or injury resulting in death occurred during commission, attempted commission or flight from commission of one of a series of specified felonies; the defendant's prior conviction for a state or federal felony involving a firearm, other than a capital offense under 18 U.S.C. §924(c) and (j); the defendant's prior conviction for a federal or state offense which resulted in death, for which life imprisonment or a death sentence was authorized by statute; the defendant's prior conviction of two or more federal or state felonies, committed on separate occasions, involving infliction or attempted infliction of serious bodily injury or death; knowing creation of grave risk of death to one or more persons other than the victim of the offense during the commission of the offense or escape from apprehension for the offense; commission of the offense in an especially heinous, cruel, or depraved manner; procurement of commission of the offense by payment or promise of payment; commission of the offense for pecuniary gain; commission of the offense after substantial planning and premeditation to cause another's death or to commit an act of terrorism; the defendant's prior conviction of two or more federal or state drug trafficking felonies; the victim's particular vulnerability due to old age,

youth or infirmity; the defendant's previous conviction of serious drug felonies under title II or III of the Comprehensive Drug Abuse Prevention and Control Act of 1970, for which sentences of at least five years of imprisonment could be imposed, or previous conviction for engaging in a continuing criminal enterprise; the defendant's commission of the offense during the course of engaging in a continuing criminal enterprise where the offense involved distribution of drugs to persons under 21; the fact that the offense was committed against certain high public officials or federal public servants (including judges, law enforcement officers, or employees of a U.S. penal or correctional institution while engaged in official duties or because of their official duties or their status as public servants); where the offense involves sexual abuse under 18 U.S.C. § 2241 *et seq.*, or sexual abuse of children under 18 U.S.C. § 2251 *et seq.*, the fact that the defendant was previously convicted of sexual assault or child molestation; or the fact that the defendant intentionally killed or attempted to kill more than one person in a single criminal episode. Aggravating factors for drug offense death penalties are set forth in 18 U.S.C. § 3592(d). These eight factors include: previous conviction of a state or federal offense involving the death of a person for which the death penalty or life imprisonment was authorized; previous conviction of two or more federal or state felonies committed on different occasions involving importation, manufacture or distribution of a controlled substance or involving the infliction of or attempted infliction of serious bodily injury or death; previous conviction of a state or federal offense involving manufacture, distribution, importation or possession of a controlled substance for which a sentence of imprisonment for five years or more was authorized; the defendant's use of a firearm in the commission of the offense or in furtherance of a continuing criminal enterprise, or the defendant's having knowingly directed, advised, authorized or assisted another to use a firearm to threaten, intimidate, assault or injure a person; the defendant directly distributed controlled substances to a person under age 21 during the commission of the offense or during a continuing criminal enterprise of which the offense was a part; the defendant directly used minors in drug trafficking during the offense or during a continuing criminal enterprise of which the offense was a part; or the defendant directly distributed controlled substances near schools during the offense or during a continuing criminal enterprise of which the offense was a part; or the offense involved the importation, manufacture, or distribution of a controlled substance mixed with a potentially lethal adulterant, where the defendant was aware of the presence of the adulterant.

[29] The statutory provisions permitting the prosecutor to propose and the jury to consider nonstatutory aggravating factors, 18 U.S.C. §§ 3592(c) and 3593(a), have withstood constitutional challenges alleging that it constituted an impermissible delegation of legislative powers to the Executive Branch. *See, e.g.*, United States v. Allen, 247 F.3d 741 (8th Cir. 2001), *vacated and remanded for reconsideration in light of Ring v. Arizona, 536 U.S. 584 (2002)*, 536 U.S. 953 (2002), *cert. denied* ___ U.S. ___, 123 S. Ct. 2273 (2003), *rehearing denied,* ___ U.S. ___, 124 S. Ct. 19 (2003), *on remand* 357 F.3d 745(8th Cir. 2004) (death sentence vacated and remanded for imposition of life sentence); *motion for rehearing en banc granted and judgment vacated*, 2004 U.S. App. LEXIS 9190 (May 11, 2004); United States v. Sampson, 275 F. Supp. 2d 49 (D. Mass. 2003). They have also passed muster under Eighth Amendment analysis, United States v. Sampson, *supra*; United States v. Frank, 8 F. Supp. 2d. 253 (S.D.N.Y. 1998) (finding that Federal Death Penalty Act did not violate the constitutional prohibition against cruel and unusual punishment by permitting nonstatutory aggravating factors); U.S. v. Llera Plaza, 179 F. Supp. 2d 444 (E.D. Pa. 2001) (holding nonstatutory aggravating factors did not permit wholly arbitrary and capricious death sentences in violation of Eighth and Fourteenth Amendments); U.S. v. Nguyen, 928 F. Supp. 1525 (D. Kan. 1996) (holding that consideration of nonstatutory aggravating factors did not result in arbitrary and capricious sentencing in violation of the Eighth Amendment); U.S. v. Sampson, *supra* (risk of execution of innocent individuals did not mean that Federal Death Penalty Act was unconstitutional under Eighth Amendment). The Federal Death penalty Act has also withstood challenges based upon the ex post facto clause, Art. I, Sec. 9, cl. 3, of the U.S. Constitution, *see*, U.S. v. Allen, *supra*; U.S. v. Frank, *supra*; U.S. v. Nguyen, *supra*; U.S. v. McVeigh, 944 F. Supp. 1478 (D. Colo. 1996); U.S. v. Chanthadara, 928 F. Supp. 1055 (D. Kan. 1996). Some cases have considered the effect of Ring v. Arizona, *supra,* upon the sufficiency of an indictment in federal death penalty cases, *see,* U.S. v. Jackson, 327 F.3d 273 (4th Cir. 2003), *cert. denied*, 540 U.S. 1019 (2003) (holding that an aggravating factor necessary to the imposition of the death penalty must be alleged in the indictment); U.S. v. Higgs, 353 F. 3d 281 (4th Cir. 2003), *cert. denied,* ___ U.S. ___, 125 S. Ct. 627 (2004) (finding that since only one aggravating factor need be found by the jury for the death penalty to be imposed under the Federal Death Penalty Act, if one statutory factor is alleged in the indictment and that aggravating factor is found by the petit jury, the indictment is not defective because it did not include all

aggravating factors that the jury might consider in determining whether to impose the death penalty); U.S. v. Regan, 221 F. Supp. 2d 672 (E.D. Va. 2002). In U.S. v. Quinones, 317 F.3d 86 (2d Cir. 2003), the court denied a motion for rehearing on an unsuccessful challenge to the Federal Death Penalty Act on the basis that the death penalty was unconstitutional per se because DNA tests had indicated that innocent people have been sentenced to death.

[30] 18 U.S.C. § 3593(b).

[31] 18 U.S.C. § 3593(c).

[32] 18 U.S.C. § 3593(d).

[33] 18 U.S.C. § 3593(e).

[34] 18 U.S.C. § 3593(f).

[35] 18 U.S.C. § 3591(b).

[36] 18 U.S.C. § 3596(b).

[37] 18 U.S.C. § 3596(c).

[38] 18 U.S.C. § 3598.

[39] 18 U.S.C. § 3595.

[40] 18 U.S.C. § 3596(a).

[41] 18 U.S.C. § 3597.

In: Capital Punishment Update
Editor: Lorraine V. Coyne, pp. 75-97
ISBN: 978-1-60456-133-3

Chapter 3

CAPITAL PUNISHMENT OVERVIEW: 2006-2007 TERM OF THE SUPREME COURT*

Paul Starett Wallace, Jr.

ABSTRACT

During its 2006-2007 term the Supreme Court announced decisions in eight capital cases. Three arose under a later abandoned Texas procedure that restricted jury consideration of mitigation evidence to evidence of intent, future dangerousness and victim provocation. In one, *Smith v. Texas*, the Court held that the defendant's failure to challenging the state's insufficient corrective adjustments in the procedure could not be used to deny him the benefit of a less demanding test to assess the harm caused by use of the challenged, defective underlying procedure. In another, *Abdul-Kabir v. Quarterman*, it rejected the suggestion that the Court's earlier cases permitted the use of the mitigating evidence-restricting procedure as long as the evidence in question related at least in part to one of the narrow factors that the procedure allowed to be considered. In the third, *Brewer v. Quarterman*, it rejected the suggestion that the Court's earlier cases permitted the use of the mitigating evidence-restricting procedure as long as the procedure permitted "sufficient" consideration of the evidence in question given its quality and weight.

Earlier in the term in *Ayers v. Belmontes*, the Court concluded that the feature in California's capital sentencing procedure that permits consideration to any evidence that extenuated the gravity of the crime

* Excerpted from CRS Report RL34100, dated July 20, 2007.

allowed a jury from giving full effect to mitigating evidence of the defendant's character and background even if otherwise unrelated to the crime.

In *Uttecht v. Brown*, the Court held that appellate courts should give considerable deference to a trial judge's dismissal of a prospective capital juror for cause. In *Schriro v. Landrigan*, it found that the absence of prejudice doomed an ineffectiveness of counsel challenge based on trial counsel's failure to search for mitigating evidence. In *Lawrence v. Florida*, it construed the federal habeas statute of limitations and concluded that the statute was not tolled pending a petition for Supreme Court review of state collateral review decisions (e.g. state habeas corpus decisions). In *Panelli v. Quarterman*, it determined that the limitation on second or successive habeas petitions posed no impediment to consideration of a petition which challenged the execution of a mentally incompetent death row inmate.

INTRODUCTION

During its 2005-2006 term, the Supreme Court announced eight capital punishment decisions, each decided by a 5-4 vote. Justice Kennedy voted with the majority in each of the eight. In the four cases in which the defendant succeeded, he joined Justices Stevens, Souter, Ginsburg and Breyer; in the four in which the state succeeded, he joined Chief Justice Roberts and Justices Scalia, Thomas and Alito. Four of the cases involved jury instructions (*Smith, Abdul-Kabir, Brewer* and *Ayers*), and a fifth (*Brown*) the selection of jurors in capital cases. Of the remaining three, one (*Landrigan*) involved an ineffectiveness of counsel challenge and the last two (*Panetti* and *Lawrence*) the application of the federal habeas corpus statute arising in a capital context.

Three cases (*Smith, Abdul-Kabir,* and *Brewer*) reopened constitutional issues on the role of juries in death penalty sentencing under a since discarded procedure in Texas and the authority of states to create their own rules for review of death cases after convictions have become final.

SMITH V. TEXAS

In *Smith v. Texas*, petitioner LaRoyce Lathair Smith was convicted of capital murder and sentenced to death by a jury in Dallas County, Texas. The trial took place in the interim between *Penry v. Lynaugh (Penry I)[1]* and *Penry v. Johnson (Penry II)*.[2] At that time, Texas capital juries were still given special issue questions that asked whether the murder had been deliberately committed, whether the defendant might prove dangerous in the future, and in cases involving a confrontation whether the defendant had been provoked.[3] If the jury found that the answer to all the special issues was yes, then the death penalty was imposed; otherwise, a sentence of life imprisonment was imposed. The special issue questions were found to be constitutionally inadequate in *Penry I* because of "the absence of instructions informing the jury that it could consider and give effect to the mitigating evidence" offered on the defendant's behalf.[4]

The Texas courts attempted to cure the inadequacy by instructing the jury that if it felt death should not be imposed but also felt the special issues were satisfied, it should falsely answer "no" to one of the special-issue questions, thus nullifying the special issues.

Prior to his trial, Smith filed three written motions addressing the jury instructions. In the first two motions, Smith argued that the special issue questions were constitutionally inadequate. In the third, Smith requested the court to state the contents of the nullification charge prior to *voir dire* in order to allow Smith to exercise his jury challenges intelligently. The trial court denied the first two motions and, in response to the third, provided Smith a copy of its proposed nullification charge. Smith raised no additional objections and did not suggest alternative wording for the nullification charge.

At sentencing, Smith's jury received the special issues questions and the supplemental "nullification instruction."[5] The instructions directed the jury to give effect to mitigation evidence, but allowed the jury to do so only by negating what would otherwise be affirmative responses to two special issues relating to deliberateness and future dangerousness. The jury sentenced Smith to death.

In his appeal and post-conviction state proceedings, Smith continued to argue his sentencing was unconstitutional because of the defects in the special issues. At each stage, the argument was either rejected on the merits, or held procedurally barred because it had already been addressed on direct appeal. Along the way, the Supreme Court in *Penry II* found the nullification charge inadequate to cure the special issues defect because of its continued failure to permit sufficient consideration of mitigating evidence.[6] The Texas Court of Criminal Appeals affirmed the denial of relief, distinguishing Smith's case from the *Penry* precedents.[7] The Supreme Court reversed, finding that there was *Penry* error and that the nullification charge was inadequate under *Penry II*.[8] On remand, the appeals court denied relief once more. Relying on its *Almanza[9]* decision, the Texas Appeals Court held that Smith had not preserved a *Penry II* challenge to the nullification charge, since he only made a *Penry I* challenge at trial and this procedural defect required him to show not merely some harm, but egregious harm, a burden he could not meet.[10]

In a decision by Justice Kennedy, the Court held: (1) that the Texas Court of Criminal Appeals made errors of federal law that cannot be the underlying basis for requiring Smith to show egregious harm; and (2) that because there is a reasonable likelihood the jury believed it was not permitted to consider Smith's relevant mitigating evidence, Smith is entitled to relief under the state harmless-error framework.

The majority opinion held that Smith's primary objection at each stage of his appeal was centered around the special issues, a *Penry I* objection.[11] As support for this conclusion, the Court's majority explained its ruling in *Smith I* as holding that the special issues prevented the jury from considering Smith's mitigating evidence, while the nullification charge simply failed to cure that error.[12] The majority was of the opinion that the Texas Court of Criminal Appeals misunderstood the interplay of *Penry I* and *Penry II* and the ruling in *Smith I*, which on remand led it to hold that by failing to object to the nullification instruction Smith had not preserved his challenge to the special issues.[13] Contrary to the belief of the Texas court, Smith was not required to object both to the fact that the special issues unconstitutionally confined jury consideration of mitigation (*Penry I*) and to the fact that the nullification instruction was an insufficient cure (*Penry II*). As a result of this error, the majority held, the Texas Court of Criminal Appeals mistakenly required Smith to show egregious harm.[14]

Having established that the Texas Court of Criminal Appeals applied the wrong standard, the majority examined Smith's claim in light of the correct standard and held that "...there was a reasonable likelihood that the jury interpreted the special issues to foreclose adequate consideration of his mitigating evidence."[15] Accordingly, the Court concluded, "it appears Smith is entitled to relief under the state harmless-error framework."[16] As a result of the Court's conclusion on this issue, the majority did not "...reach the question [of] whether the nullification charge resulted in a separate jury-confusion error, and if so, whether that error is subject to harmless-error review."[17]

The dissenting opinion written by Justice Alito and joined by Chief Justice Roberts, Justices Scalia, and Thomas concluded that the judgment of the Texas Court of Criminal Appeals on remand did not conflict with the Court's mandate in *Smith I.[18]* More specifically, the dissent took issue with the majority's conclusion that Smith had preserved his objection and, as a result, would have held that the Texas Court of Criminal Appeals correctly applied the egregious harm standard. Although Smith did argue that the special issues precluded the jury from considering mitigating evidence, by failing to argue that the trial judge's proposed instructions were insufficient to cure that defect, according to the dissent, Smith failed to preserve his claim.[19] The dissent further stated that the majority's contrary conclusion was tantamount to holding that Smith "had a federal right to sandbag the trial court."[20]

Distinguishing a prior ruling of the Texas Court of Criminal Appeals in *Smith I*, the dissenters said the state court never held that Smith's challenge was properly preserved; therefore, despite having previously rejected the federal claim on the merits, the state court was not precluded from imposing the state law procedural bar on remand of *Smith I.[21]* Also, the dissent concluded that the "'egregious harm' standard [was] an adequate and independent state ground sufficient to support a state judgement that precludes consideration of a federal right."[22]

BREWER AND ABDUL-KABIR V. QUARTERMAN

Abdul-Kabir [Cole] v. Quarterman[23] concerns habeas corpus rulings of the U.S. Court of Appeals for the Fifth Circuit arising out of the Texas "special issues" procedure. *Brewer v. Quarterman[24]* is its companion. Similar to *Smith v. Texas*,[25] the cases address the question of whether the instructions given to inmate Brewer's and inmate Abdul-Kabir's juries provided a sufficient vehicle for consideration of the mitigating evidence presented. The statutory scheme under which they were sentenced was ruled unconstitutional in 1989 in *Penry I*.[26] In 1991, the Texas legislature amended the statute to correct the deficiency. The pre-1991cases (Smith, Brewer and Abdul-Kabir), however, continued to proceed through the courts, while the Supreme Court issued three more decisions involving Texas cases in an effort to enforce their original ruling. These cases were *Penry v. Johnson* (*Penry II*),[27] *Smith v. Texas* (*Smith I*)[28] and *Tennard v. Dretke*.[29]

While Abdul-Kabir's habeas case was pending initially, the Court in *Tennard* rejected a Fifth Circuit standard under which for purposes of certain *Penry* claims a prisoner was required to demonstrate a nexus between the mitigating evidence and the offense of conviction.[30] The Court remanded Abdul-Kabir for reconsideration in light of *Tennard.[31]* On remand, the Fifth Circuit denied habeas relief on the grounds that the special issue questions permitted the jury to honestly consider the mitigating effect of the particular evidence in the case. They therefore concluded the state court decisions regarding the use of the special issue questions were not contrary to Supreme Court precedent, because the deliberateness and future danger questions permitted the jury to consider mitigating evidence of a destructive family background and a neurological condition deficiency.[32] It reached much the same conclusion in Brewer's case; the jury could consider depression, substance abuse and destructive family background when called upon to answer the deliberateness and future dangerousness questions.[33] In fact, it suggested that Brewer's claim was less robust, quantitatively and qualitatively, than Abdul-Kabir's.[34] The Supreme Court granted certiorari and consolidated the cases for argument.[35] It then reversed in separate opinions.[36]

The Court decided in *Abdul-Kabir* that the Fifth Circuit wrongly applied the *Penry* line of cases and its predecessors when it concluded that the Texas court decisions were not clearly contrary to existing Court precedents. Writing for the majority, Justice Stevens said their cases beginning with *Lockett v. Ohio[37]* and continuing through *Penry I* have been "... clear that when the jury is not permitted to give meaningful effect or a 'reasonable moral response' to a defendant's mitigating evidence – because it is forbidden from doing so by statute or a judicial interpretation of a statute – the sentencing process is fatally flawed."[38]

Chief Justice Roberts and Justices Alito, Scalia, and Thomas dissented. Chief Justice Roberts for the dissenters said the majority should have deferred to lower court rulings against the defendants because in light of facially limiting, contemporaneous Court decisions there was no clearly established federal law that judges could have followed to grant relief.[39] Justices Scalia and Thomas added a separate dissent in which they repeated their view that mitigating evidence may be kept from the jury without constitutional offense and bemoaned the want of Supreme Court consistency on the question.[40]

The separate opinion in *Brewer* appears to have been designed to preclude any indication that the special issue procedure may have continued vitality in those cases in which they permit the jury to give "sufficient effect" to the defendant's evidence when the defendant's unassessed mitigating evidence is less robust than that available in *Penry* or *Abdul-Kabir*.[41] No more acceptable to the majority than its "constitutional relevance" theory is the Fifth Circuit's suggestion that a jury has given "sufficient effect" to mitigating evidence whose impact largely falls within the special issues' sphere of relevance even though some lesser mitigating effects may be disregarded simple because they fall beyond its edge.[42]

AYERS S. BELMONTES

In *Ayers v. Belmontes*,[43] decided November 13, 2006, a California jury convicted Belmontes of murder, and sentenced him to death. Belmontes argued that part of the jury instruction violated the Eight Amendment by keeping the jury from considering evidence that would have a bearing on how he would behave as a prisoner if he were sentenced to prison rather than sentenced to death.

A California statute states that the jury can consider several mitigating factors when considering whether to impose the death penalty. One of these is "factor (k)" which is "any other circumstance which extenuates the gravity of the crime even though it is not a legal excuse for the crime." After being sentenced to death, Belmontes argued at the California Supreme Court that the jury instructions which incorporated factor (k) prevented the jury from considering background evidence unless that evidence related to the murder itself. The California court upheld the conviction.[44] Belmontes then filed a federal *habeas corpus* petition raising the same argument, and the Ninth Circuit decided in his favor.[45] California challenged the ruling and after remand from the U.S. Supreme Court, the Ninth Circuit again held in favor of Belmontes and for the same reasons.[46] In another 5-4 decision, the Supreme Court reinstated the death penalty, concluding that factor (k)'s reference to any evidence which extenuated the gravity of the crime allowed a jury from giving full effect to mitigating evidence of the defendant's character and background even if otherwise unrelated to the crime.[47] "It was mistaken...to find a 'reasonable probability' that the jury did not consider respondent's future potential," Justice Kennedy wrote.[48] Chief Justice Roberts and Justices Alito, Scalia, and Thomas joined Justice Kennedy's opinion.

In his dissent, Justice Stevens said the majority opinion reaches a "strange conclusion" based upon speculation.[49]

UTTECHT V. BROWN

On June 4, 2007, the Court in *Uttecht v. Brown[50]* decided that the Washington state trial judge who presided over the trial of Cal Coburn Brown properly used his discretion to excuse a potential juror who had expressed mixed views regarding the death penalty.[51] After the Washington Supreme Court upheld the trial judge's dismissal of the juror,[52] the federal district court denied Brown's *habeas* petition. The defendant requested *habeas corpus* relief in the U.S. Court of Appeals for the Ninth Circuit and the Court of Appeals reversed finding that under *Witherspoon v. Illinois[53]* the trial court had violated Brown's Sixth and Fourteenth Amendment rights by excusing Juror Z for cause on the ground that he could not be impartial in deciding whether to impose a death sentence.[54] The Court of Appeals said that excluding a juror is allowed only if it is clear that the juror would not follow the law. The Court of Appeals noted that the juror should not have been excused because he said he would consider the death penalty in an appropriate case.[55]

However, the Supreme Court reinstated the death sentence of Brown based on the premise that the Court of Appeals should have given deference to the trial judge because determinations of a juror's demeanor and credibility are within his province.[56] Writing for the majority, Justice Kennedy said "...where, as here, there is lengthy questioning of a prospective juror and the trial court has supervised a diligent and thoughtful *voir dire* [examination], the trial court has broad discretion."[57]

Dissenting, Justice Stevens, said the Court wiped away earlier decisions that allow death penalty opponents to sit on juries in capital cases, provided they demonstrate that they can set aside their "beliefs in deference to the rule of law."[58] Justice Stevens noted that juror Z was struck for cause although she was not necessarily an opponent of the death penalty since on *voir dire* (examination), she said she could impose the death penalty if convinced that it was the appropriate measure.[59] Justices Breyer, Souter, and Ginsburg also dissented.

SCHRIROV. LANDRIGAN

In *Schriro v. Landrigan*,[60] decided by the Court on May 14, 2007, the respondent, Jeffrey Landrigan was convicted and sentenced to death for murder committed during a burglary.[61] At sentencing, he undermined his attorney's effort to develop and present any mitigating evidence. His attorney sought to offer the testimony of his mother and ex-wife as mitigating evidence; Landrigan persuaded them not to testify.[62] He informed the court that he had instructed his attorney not to present mitigating evidence and that as far as he was concerned there were no mitigating circumstances.[63] His attorney sought to assert that Landrigan had been lawfully employed to support his family; he interjected that he was "doing robberies supporting my family" as well.[64] His attorney suggested the stabbing of a fellow inmate may have been self-defense; he would have none of it and ended the effort with the observation that "I stabbed him 14 times. It was lucky he lived. But two weeks later they found him hung in his cell."[65]

The court sentenced Landrigan to death and his direct appeals proved unsuccessful.[66] Landrigan then filed an ineffective assistance claim first in state court and then in federal court.[67] Landrigan argued that if his lawyer had explained better, he would have agreed to allow him at his sentencing hearing to present evidence that he suffered because of fetal alcohol syndrome and a history of violence in his biological family.[68] The Arizona Supreme Court, the U.S. District Court for the District of Arizona, and a three-judge panel of the Court of Appeals for the Ninth Circuit all rejected Landrigan's argument. However, the Ninth Circuit Court of Appeals en banc affirmed in part, reversed in part, and remanded, saying Landrigan was entitled to a hearing on his claim that his lawyer was ineffective.[69]

In the eyes of the en banc panel, Landrigan's trial attorney conducted almost no investigation for sentencing and certainly no probing investigation.[70] At the sentencing hearing, Landrigan simply told the court that he did not wish for his mother or ex-wife to testify on his behalf. And trial counsel was unprepared to present any other witnesses. Landrigan knew of no other mitigating evidence because his attorney had developed none. When the state courts found that his instruction not to use his mother and ex-wife to present mitigating evidence constituted an instruction not to present any mitigating evidence from any other source, they had engaged in an unreasonable determination of the facts, as far as the panel was concerned.[71] During habeas corpus proceedings in the district court, mitigating evidence was developed showing organic brain damage, fetal alcohol, and certain genetic predispositions.[72] None of this evidence was developed by trial counsel. Moreover, Landrigan had shown no want of diligence to develop the factual basis for his claim.[73] The post-conviction counsel asked for funding for experts and an evidentiary hearing. The state objected to both and the state court denied funding and a hearing.[74] The Supreme Court granted the state's petition for certiorari[75] and reversed.[76]

The ultimate weakness of Landrigan's argument and the en banc decision, in the opinion of the Court, was weakness of the unheard mitigating evidence. Justice Thomas, writing for the Court with the concurrence of four of his brethren, pointed out that habeas relief may only be granted if the state court's treatment of the claim constitutes either unreasonable application of federal law or an unreasonable application of the facts to that law.[77] A court need conduct an evidentiary hearing in aid of an effort to overcome these obstacles, explained the Court, when "the petition's factual allegations ... if true, would entitle the applicant to federal habeas relief."[78] Here, the claim of ineffective assistance of counsel would require a showing of a "deficient performance by counsel *resulting in prejudice*."[79] As far as the Court was concerned, the district court that denied habeas relief "did not abuse its discretion in finding that Landrigan could not establish prejudice based on his counsel's failure to present the evidence he now wishes to offer."[80]

The Court's treatment of the contrary en banc panel decision is straightforward in some respects and instructive in others. It concluded that based on the record the panel was simply wrong when it characterized as an unreasonable determination of the facts the state court holdings that Landrigan had instructed his trial attorney not to offer any mitigating evidence.[81] "The Arizona court's determination that Landrigan refused to allow the presentation of any mitigating evidence was a reasonable determination of the facts," said Justice Thomas.[82]

The Court's terse rebuttal of two other points found in the en banc decision may prove more revealing of the Court's future direction. First, the panel suggested that Landrigan's conduct "cannot excuse his counsel's failure to conduct an adequate investigation prior to the sentencing." Earlier cases seemed to teach: (1) in *Wiggins*, that the adequacy of a presentencing investigation is measured at the time the investigation was and should have been conducted not at the time of sentencing hearing;[83] and (2) in *Rompilla*, that counsel must sometimes probe the defendant's background for mitigating evidence even when the defendant and members of his family assure counsel there is none.[84] The Court dismissed the references with the observation that it had never previously addressed "a situation in which a client interferes with counsel's efforts to present mitigating evidence to a sentencing court."[85] No more need have been said since a habeas court may not distribute a state court's ruling on the merits of a claim in absence of contrary Supreme Court precedent.[86] Yet this does little to encourage the belief that the Court may soon address the question and resolve it to the possible benefit of state death row inmates.

The want of Supreme Court precedent was but one of several reasons why the Court was unmoved by the panel's objection that any decision of Landrigan's to forego the introduction of mitigating evidence could hardly be described as "informed and knowing."[87] The Court has "never imposed an 'informed and knowing' requirement upon a defendant's decision not to introduce evidence."[88] Even if such a claim had merit, Landrigan could not assert it because he had failed to present to state courts first.[89] In addition, the Court noted that trial counsel had in fact alluded to the perils of Landrigan's decision to bar the introduction of mitigating evidence.[90] Finally, Landrigan dispelled any illusion that he was unaware of the consequences of unheard mitigating evidence when in his final statement he told the sentencing judge, "I think if you want to give the death penalty, just bring it right on. I'm ready for it."[91]

Again, the Court did little to encourage the belief that it would soon rule and rule in a manner favorable to defendants on the question of whether a capital defendant may only waive the introduction of mitigating evidence at sentencing if his decision is an informed and knowing one.

Justice Stevens, writing the dissent, said the Court should have allowed the hearing to determine whether Landrigan truly did not want a judge to consider evidence in his favor as well as the strength of mitigating factors.[92] "Without the benefit of an evidentiary hearing, this is pure guesswork," Justice Stevens said.[93]

Furthermore, Justice Stevens continued, in light of a panoply of circumstances under which the Court has held that trial rights may only be intelligently waived, "it makes little difference that we have not specifically imposed an informed and knowing requirement upon a defendant's decision not to introduce evidence. A capital defendant's right to present mitigating evidence is firmly established and can only be exercised at a sentencing trial."[94]

Finally, the dissenters could not accept the majority's conclusion that Landrigan's mitigating evidence was weak or that it could be said without hearing that Landrigan had not been prejudiced by his trial counsel's failure to investigate the presence, depth and breath of any mitigating evidence.[95]

LAWRENCE V. FLORIDA

On February 20, 2007, the Supreme Court announced its decision in *Lawrence v. Florida[96]* seeking to address the confusion surrounding the tolling of a one-year statute of limitations applicable to federal *habeas corpus* petitions. The statute provides for tolling through "the conclusion of direct appeal" including certiorari review by the Supreme Court.[97] It provides for tolling thereafter during the "pendency of state post-conviction or other collateral review" (i.e., habeas in state court).[98] But does this include the period during pendency of a petition for Supreme Court certiorari review of this second round of state proceedings. Prior to *Lawrence,* a split had developed in the circuits on the question. On one hand, the Eleventh Circuit and others held that the statute of limitations was not tolled during the pendency of a certiorari petition to the Supreme Court seeking review of a state court's collateral relief decision.[99] On the other hand, the Sixth Circuit decided differently prior to *Lawrence*, concluding that an application for state post-conviction relief would remain pending and would therefore toll the statute of limitations during the review by the Supreme Court.[100]

In settling the issue, the Court, in a 5-4 decision with Justice Thomas writing for the majority (which Chief Justice Roberts and Justices Scalia, Kennedy and Alito joined) rejected the Sixth Circuit reasoning and affirmed that of the Eleventh Circuit. The majority opinion decided that under ordinary circumstances, the time to file under the Antiterrorism and Effective Death Penalty Act of 1996 (AEDPA) is not tolled while the Court is considering whether to grant *certiorari* regarding a state post-conviction petition; tolling of the statute of limitations is available only during direct appeals including certiorari to the Supreme Court and then during the pendency of the state post-conviction proceedings in state court, but not during the pendency of a petition for Supreme Court review of those proceedings.[101] For the majority, the issue turned on the language used in the statute. Supreme Court review cannot be part of the "state" review to which Congress referred when it spoke of "state post-conviction or other collateral review" in paragraph 2244(d)(2).[102] That phrase, Justice Thomas continued, stands in stark contrast to the phrase used in paragraph 2244(d)(1) that contemplates Supreme Court participation as the final stage of the state appellate process – "the conclusion of direct review."[103]

Justice Ginsburg with whom Justices Stevens, Souter, and Breyer joined in dissenting would hold that 28 U.S.C. § 2244(d)'s statue of limitations is tolled during the pendency of a petition for certiorari to review of state collateral relief opinions.[104] The dissent concluded that the language does not require, nor should practicality encourage, a statutory construction that would compel a state prisoner to file his habeas petition in federal district court while his petition requesting review of the very same issues is pending before the Supreme Court.[105]

PANETTI V. QUARTERMAN

On the last day of its term, the Supreme Court announced its decision in *Panetti v. Quarterman*.[106] The questions presented were: "(1) Does the Eighth Amendment permit the execution of a death row inmate who has a factual awareness of the reason for his execution but who, because of severe mental illness, has a delusional belief as to why the state of Texas is executing him, and thus does not comprehend that his execution is intended to seek punishment for his capital crime? (2) Does the Antiterrorism and Effective Death Penalty Act of 1996 (AEDPA) require deference to the state court's determination that Panetti is competent to be executed–and thereby statutorily preclude Panetti's request for federal *habeas* relief? and (3) Must petitioner's habeas application be dismissed as 'second or successive' pursuant to 28 U.S.C. 2244?"[107]

In 1995, Panetti was convicted of capital murder and sentenced to death by a Texas jury for the 1992 slaying of his in-laws in the presence of his wife and three-year-old daughter.[108] Following his direct appeal, state post-conviction proceedings, and initial efforts at federal *habeas* relief were all unsuccessful, an execution date was set.[109] In December 2003, Panetti claimed for the first time that he was mentally incompetent to be executed. Other procedural maneuvers followed his claim, however, in May 2004, the state trial court (relying on evaluations by court-appointed experts) decided that Panetti was competent.[110] The state court then closed the case without ruling on various pending motions filed by Panetti, including requests for a competency hearing and for funds to hire his own expert.[111]

Panetti went back to federal court, where a second *habeas* petition was pending. The district court held that although the state court had not complied with either state law or the requirements imposed by the Supreme Court's decision in *Ford v. Wainright*,[112] Panetti was competent as defined by Fifth Circuit precedent insofar as he was aware of his impending execution and the basis for the execution.[113] The Fifth Circuit affirmed,[114] and the Supreme Court granted certiorari.[115]

On June28, 2007, the Court in a 5-4 ruling reversed the Fifth Circuit. First, the Court rejected the state's argument that the Court lacked jurisdiction to consider the case because Panetti's first federal *habeas* petition would, explained the Court, prompt all death row inmates to include such claims in their first petition even though the claims may not be ripe or meritless.[116] While announcing what appears to be a new rule,[117] the Court concluded that "Congress did not intend the provisions of AEDPA addressing 'second or successive' petitions to govern a filing in the unusual posture presented here: a § 2254 application raising a *Ford*-based incompetency claim filed as soon as that claim is ripe."[118] Notwithstanding, the lower courts here emphasized instead, "[a]n empty formality requiring prisoners to file unripe *Ford* claims [which] neither respects the limited resources available to the States nor encourages the exhaustion of state remedies."[119] Recognizing that the State's argument had some merit, nonetheless, Justice Kennedy concluded that it was flawed because of "[t]he results it would produce"[120] when considered with an earlier decision.[121]

The Court addressed the next issue that, in the state's opinion, would preclude it from reaching the merits of Panetti's claim regarding the state court's determination that Panetti was competent and was entitled to deference under the

AEDPA.[122] The Court agreed with Panetti that no deference was due because the state court had failed to provide Panetti with the minimum procedures required by Justice Powell's concurring opinion in *Ford*–which, the Court explained constituted "clearly established law" for AEDPA purposes.[123] The Court took notice that in Panetti's case, for example, the state court failed to provide Panetti with even the "rudimentary process" of giving him an opportunity to submit psychiatric evidence to rebut the report filed by the court-appointed experts.[124] The Court left undecided questions regarding other due process protections – "such as the opportunity for discovery or the cross-examination of witnesses which may also be required.[125] The Court rejected any idea that the state court's application of *Ford* was necessarily reasonable because the standard outlined in *Ford* was "stated in general terms": "AEDPA does not require state and federal courts to wait for some nearly identical factual pattern before a legal rule must be applied. Nor does AEDPA prohibit a federal court from finding an application of a principle unreasonable when it involves a set of facts 'different from those in which the principle was announced.'"[126]

Lastly, the Court addressed the merits of Panetti's Eighth Amendment claim. The Court considered the Fifth Circuit's test "too restrictive" insofar as it "treats a prisoner's delusional belief system as irrelevant if the prisoner knows that the state has identified his crimes as the reason for his execution."[127] In the Court's opinion, "[a] prison's awareness of the State's rational for an execution is not the same as a rational understanding of it. *Ford* does not foreclose the latter."[128]

In the dissent joined by Chief Justice Roberts and Justices Scalia and Alito, Justice Thomas said "[t]his case should be simple" because Panetti's claim does not meet AEDPA's "'second or successive' *habeas* application" requirements.[129] According to Justice Thomas, "...the Court ben[t] over backwards to allow Panetti to bring his Ford claim despite no evidence that his condition has worsened – or even changed – since 1995."[130] Referring to the Court's earlier decision in *Burton v. Stewart*,[131] Justice Thomas said "[i]n light of *Burton*, it simply cannot be maintained that Panetti is excused from § 2244's requirements solely because his *Ford* claim would have been unripe had he included it in his first *habeas* application."[132] The dissent, according to Justice Thomas, minimizes the majority's opinion as representing only "the proposition that *Ford* claims somehow deserve a special (and unjustified) exemption from the statute's plain import."[133]

REFERENCES

[1] 492 U.S. 302 (1989) (*Penry I*).
[2] 532 U.S. 782 (2001) (*Penry II*).
[3] More exactly, "(1) Whether the conduct of the defendant that caused the death of the deceased was committed deliberately and with the reasonable expectation that the death of the deceased would result; (2) whether there is a probability that the defendant would commit criminal acts of violence that would constitute a continuing threat; and (3) if raised by the evidence, whether the conduct of the defendant ibn killing the deceased was unreasonable in response to the provocation, if any, by the deceased," Tex. Code Crim. Pro. art. 37.071(b)(1981 ed. and Supp. 1989).
[4] 492 U.S. at 328.
[5] *Ex parte Smith,* 132 S.W.3d 407, 409 (Tex. Crim. App. 2004).
[6] "Any realistic assessment of the manner in which the supplemental instruction operated would therefore lead to the same conclusion we reached in *Penry I*: '[A] reasonable juror could well have believed that there was no vehicle for expressing the view that Penry did not deserve to be sentenced to death based upon his mitigating evidence,'" 532 U.S. at 804.
[7] 132 S.W.3d at 413.
[8] *Smith v. Texas*, 543 U.S. 37 (2004) (*Smith I*).
[9] *Almanza v. State*, 686 S.W.2d 157 (Tex. Crim. App. 1984 (*en banc*)).
[10] *Ex parte Smith,* 185 S.W.3d 455, 463-64 (Tex. Crim. App. 2006). Under the *Almanza* standard, when a defendant challenges a jury instruction the court must determine whether there was error in the jury charge, and if so, whether the defendant objected at the time. If the defendant failed to object "he must show that the error caused him such egregious harm that he did not have a 'fair and impartial trial.'" *Id.* at 463.
[11] 127 S. Ct. at 1697.
[12] *Id.* at 1691.
[13] *Id.* at 1698.
[14] Id.
[15] *Id.* at 1698.
[16] *Id.* at 1699.
[17] Id.
[18] *Id.* at 1706.
[19] *Id.* at 1704-1705
[20] *Id.* at 1702.
[21] *Id.* at 1702-1703.

[22] *Id.* at 1704-1705.

[23] 127 S. Ct. 1654, 1660-1662 (2007). (In 1987, Jalil Abdul-Kabir was convicted of capital murder after he confessed to strangling 66-year-old Raymond Richardson with a dog leash to steal $20.00 from him. At sentencing, the trial judge asked the jury to answer two special issues, affirmative answer to which would require the judge to impose a death sentence: whether Abdul-Kabir's conduct was committed deliberately and with the reasonable expectation it would result in his victim's death and whether it was probable he would commit future violent acts constituting a continuing threat to society. Abdul-Kabir's mitigating evidence included family members' testimony describing his unhappy childhood as well as expert testimony which, to some extent, contradicted the State's claim that he was dangerous. However, the prosecutor discouraged the jurors from taking these matters into account, advising them instead to answer the special issues based only on the facts and to disregard any other views as to what might constitute an appropriate punishment for this particular defendant).

[24] 127 S. Ct. 1706, 1710-1711 (2007). (Petitioner Brewer was convicted of murder committed during the course of a robbery. At sentencing, he introduced mitigating evidence of his mental illness, his father's extensive abuse of him and his mother, and his substance abuse. "In closing argument, the prosecutor emphasized that Brewer's violent response to physical abuse by his father supported an affirmative answer to the 'future dangerousness' special issue. In contrast, he de-emphasize any mitigating effect such evidence should have ..." saying, "'you know, folks, you can take a puppy, and you can beat the puppy and you can make him mean, but if that dog bites, he is going to bite the rest of his life.'" Moreover, he told the jurors that they "lacked the power to exercise moral judgment in determining Brewer's sentence." Ultimately, the jury answered both special issues in the affirmative, and Brewer was sentenced to death.).

[25] 127 S. Ct. 1686 (2007).

[26] *Penry v. Lynaugh*, 492 U.S. 302 (1989).

[27] 532 U.S. 782 (2001).

[28] 543 U.S. 37 (2004).

[29] 542 U.S. 274 (2004).

[30] "The court began by stating the test applied in the Fifth Circuit to *Penry* claims, which involves a threshold inquiry into whether the petitioner presented 'constitutionally relevant' mitigating evidence of a 'uniquely severe permanent handicap with which the defendant was burdened through

no fault of his own,' and evidence that 'the criminal act was attributable to his severe permanent condition." *Id.* at 281. "The Fifth Circuit's test has no foundation in the decisions of this Court," *Id.* at 284.

[31] *Abdul-Kabir v. Dretke*, 543 U.S. 985 (2004).

[32] *Cole v. Dretke*, 418 F.3d 494, 505-11 (5th Cir. 2005).

[33] *Brewer v. Dretke*, 442 F.3d 273, 279-82 (5th Cir. 2006).

[34] "In *Coble* and *Cole*, moreover, the record contained expert psychiatric evidence that bore both on the defendant's future dangerousness and other potential issues relating to mental impairment. Even if Brewer [who failed to offer the testimony of expert witnesses] had proved mental illness (which it appears he did not), and even if mental illness were tantamount to mental retardation for the purposes of our case law (which it is not), Brewer came nowhere near to producing evidence sufficient for us to grant relief," 442 F.3d at 281.

[35] *Abdul-Kabir v. Quarterman*, 127 S.Ct. 432 (2006); *Brewer v. Quarterman*, 127 S.Ct.433 (2006).

[36] *Abdul-Kabir v. Quarterman*, 127 S.Ct. 1654 (2007); *Brewer v. Quarterman*, 127 S.Ct.1706 (2007). The dissents in the two opinions, however, are identical, 127 S.Ct. at 1675, 1684; 127 S.Ct. at 1713, 1723.

[37] 438 U.S. 586 (1978).

[38] 127 U.S. at 1665-1671.

[39] *Id.* at 1681-1682, citing *inter alia*, *Graham v. Collins*, 506 U.S. 461 (1993) and *Johnson v. Texas*, 509 U.S. 350 (1993).

[40] 127 S.Ct. at 1684-1686.

[41] "Nowhere in our *Penry* line of cases have we suggested that the question whether mitigating evidence could have been adequately considered by the jury is a matter purely of quantity, degree, or immutability. Rather, we have focused on whether such evidence has mitigating relevance to the special issues and the extent to which it may diminish a defendant's moral culpability for the crime," 127 S.Ct. at 1712-1713.

[42] "[T]he Court of Appeals mischaracterized the law as demanding only that such evidence be given 'sufficient mitigating effect,' and improperly equated 'sufficient effect' with 'fully effect.' . . . Like the 'constitution relevance' standard that we rejected in *Tennard*, a 'sufficient effect' standard has 'no foundation in the decisions of this Court,'" *Id.* at 1713.

[43] 127 S. Ct. 469 (2006).

[44] *People v. Belmontes,* 755 P.2d 310 (Cal. 1988), *certiorari* denied in *Belmontes v. California,* 488 U.S. 1034 (1989).

[45] *Belmontes v. Woodford,* 350 F.3d 861 (9th Cir. 2003), vacated and remand for reconsideration in light of *Brown v. Payton, Brown v. Belmontes*, 544 U.S. 945 (2005). *Brown v. Payton*, 544 U.S. 133, 142 (2005), held that the California Supreme Court had not ruled contrary to U.S. Supreme Court precedent when it held factor (k) would not lead a reasonable jury in a capital case to conclude that it must disregard mitigating evidence of a defendant's subsequent rehabilitation.

[46] *Belmontes v. Brown,* 414 F.3d 1094 (9th Cir. 2005).

[47] 127 S.Ct. at 473-74, describing *Boyde v. California*, 494 U.S. 370 (1990).

[48] *Ayers v. Belmontes,* 127 S. Ct. 469, 475 (2006).

[49] *Id.* at 492.

[50] 127 S. Ct. 2218 (2007).

[51] *Id.* at 2228.

[52] *State v. Brown*, 132 Wash.2d 529, 940 P.2d 546 (1997).

[53] 391 U.S. 510 (1968) (In an opinion written by Justice Potter Stewart, the Court held 6-3 that Witherspoon's death sentence was unconstitutional. The Court reasoned that a jury composed after the dismissal of all who oppose the death sentence was biased in favor of the death sentence; such a jury was not impartial and thus violated the Sixth and Fourteenth Amendments. The Court held that while jurors who say they will not impose the death sentence can be dismissed; jurors who merely oppose the death sentence as a personal belief may not. Justice William Douglas, concurring, was of the opinion that it is also unconstitutional to dismiss prospective jurors who say they will never impose the death sentence.).

[54] The Circuit Court depicted the consideration of the Juror Z's dismissal for cause as follows: "Z expressed no antipathy toward the death penalty; to the contrary, he stated that he 'believe[d] in the death penalty.'In explaining his views, Z outlined a balanced and thoughtful position. For example, Z was discomforted by an earlier era in which '[i]t seemed like ... [the death penalty] wasn't used at all,' because he believed 'there [a]re times when it would be appropriate [to impose the death penalty].' But he expressed caution that the death penalty be reserved for 'severe situations': 'I don't think it should never happen, and I don't think it should happen 10 times a week either.' Z felt most comfortable imposing the death penalty where the defendant is 'incorrigible and would reviolate if released,' and less comfortable where the defendant is found to have been 'temporarily insane.' But he stated unequivocally that he could consider the death penalty as an option if told to do so. ... More importantly, he promised he would 'follow the law' without reservation. Despite these assurances, the prosecutor

protested that Z was too reluctant to impose the death penalty, and that he would only vote for death if convinced that the defendant would 'kill again.' The prosecutor thus moved to excuse juror Z for cause, and the trial judge granted the motion without further inquiry," *Brown v. Lambert*, 451 F.3d 946, 949 (2006).

[55] 451 F.3d at 950-953.

[56] 127 S.Ct. at 2228.

[57] *Id.* at 2230.

[58] *Id.* at 2240.

[59] *Id.* at 2239.

[60] 127 S. Ct. 1933 (2007).

[61] Landrigan had previously stabbed and attempted to murder a fellow inmate while serving time for an earlier murder. *Id.* at 1937.

[62] *Id.* at 1937.

[63] Id.

[64] Id.

[65] *Landrigan v. Stewart*, 272 F.3d 1221, 1227 (9th Cir. 2001).

[66] *State v. Landrigan*, 176 Ariz. 1, 859 P.2d 111 (1993).

[67] *Id.* at 1223-1224.

[68] Id.

[69] *Landrigan v. Schriro*, 441 F.3d 638, 642 (9th Cir. 2006).

[70] *Id.* at 643-646.

[71] *Id.* at 646-647. In state prisoner cases, the federal statute binds federal habeas courts to state court decisions with two exceptions, one of which is that the state court decision "was based on an unreasonable determination of the facts in light of the evidence presented in the state court proceeding." 28 U.S.C. 2254(d)(2). Under 28 U.S.C. 2254(e)(1) state court findings of fact are presumed correct absent a contrary showing by clear and convincing evidence.

[72] *Id.* at 648-649.

[73] *Id.* Again in state prisoner cases, the statute declares that a petitioner who has previously failed to develop the factual basis for his claim may have an evidentiary hearing to do so only under two circumstances, one of which is that "the factual predicate that could not have been previously discovered through the exercise of due diligence." 28 U.S.C. 2254(e)(2)(A) (ii). Even with this accomplished, he must also demonstrate "by clear and convincing evidence that but for the constitutional error," such as the ineffective assistance of counsel, "no reasonable fact-finder would have found the

applicant guilty of the underlying offense" or subject to the challenged penalty. 28 U.S.C. 2254(e)(2)(B).

[74] *Id.*at 642-643.

[75] *Landrigan v. Schriro*, 127 S.Ct. 35 (2006).

[76] 127 S.Ct. at 1944.

[77] 127 S.Ct. at 1939, citing, 28 U.S.C. 2554(d)(1),(2).

[78] *Id.* at 1940.

[79] *Rompilla v. Beard*, 545 U.S. 374, 380 (2005)(emphasis added), citing, *Strickland v. Washington*, 466 U.S. 668, 687 (1984). The Court seems to take for granted without saying as much that habeas relief under *Strickland* requires a showing of *prejudicial* ineffective assistance, see, 127 S.Ct. at 1941 ("the District Court could conclude that because of his established recalcitrance, Landrigan could not demonstrate prejudice under *Strickland* even if granted an evidentiary hearing. The Court of Appeals offered two addition reasons for holding that Landrigan's inability to make a showing of prejudice under *Strickland* did not bar any potential habeas relief ... it was not objectively unreasonable for that court to conclude that a defendant who refused to allow the presentation of any mitigating evidence could not establish *Strickland* prejudice... .").

[80] *Id.* at 1943-1944. (The Court continued, "Landrigan's mitigation evidence was weak, and the postconviction court was well acquainted with Landrigan's exceedingly violent past and had seen first hand his belligerent behavior. Again, it is difficult to improve upon the initial Court of Appeals panel's conclusion: 'The prospect was chilling: before he was 30 years of age, Landrigan had murdered one man, repeatedly stabbed another one, escaped from prison, and within two months murdered still another man. ... In his comments to the sentencing judge, defendant not only failed to show remorse or offer mitigating evidence, but he flaunted his menacing behavior. On this record, assuring the court that genetics made him the way he is could not have been very helpful. There was no prejudice.' 272 F.3d at 1229.").

[81] 127 S.Ct. at 1940-1941.

[82] *Id.* at 1941. In addition, the district court, whose denial habeas relief the panel overturned, "was entitled to conclude that regardless of what information counsel might have uncovered in his investigation, Landrigan would have interrupted and refused to allow his counsel to present any such evidence." *Id.* at 1942.

[83] *Wiggins v. Smith*, 539 U.S. 510, 522-23 (2003)(emphasis in the original)("In finding Williams' ineffectiveness claim meritorious, we applied *Strickland*

and concluded that counsel's failure to uncover and present voluminous mitigating evidence at sentencing could not be justified as a tactical decision ... because counsel had not fulfilled their obligation to conduct a thorough investigation of the defendant's background. ...[O]ur principal concern ... is not whether counsel should have presented a mitigation case. Rather, we focus on whether the investigation supporting counsel's decision not to introduce mitigating evidence of Wiggins' background *was itself reasonable*.").

[84] *Rompilla v. Beard*, 545 U.S. 374, 383 (2005)("The Commonwealth argues that the information trial counsel gathered from Rompilla and the other sources gave them sound reason to think it would have been pointless to spend time and money on the additional investigation espoused by postconviction counsel, and we can say that there is room for debate about trial counsel's obligation to follow at least some of those potential lines of enquiry").

[85] 127 S.Ct. at 1942.

[86] 28 U.S.C. 2254(d).

[87] 441 F.3d at 647 ("Nor does the record indicate that Landrigan's decision was informed and knowing. It is difficult for an attorney to advise a client of the prospects of success or the potential consequences of failing to present mitigating evidence when the attorney does not know that such evidence exists").

[88] 127 S.Ct. at 1942.

[89] *Id.* at 1942-1943, citing, 28 U.S.C. 2254(e)(2).

[90] *Id.* at 1943 ("[I]n Landrigan's presence, his counsel told the sentencing court that he had carefully explained to Landrigan the importance of mitigating evidence, especially concerning the fact that state is seeking the death penalty.").

[91] Id.

[92] *Id.* at 1955.

[93] *Id.* at 1944.

[94] *Id.* at 1947.

[95] *Id.* at 1953-1954.

[96] 127 S. Ct. 1079 (2007).

[97] 28 U.S.C. 2244(d)(1).

[98] 28 U.S.C. 2244(d)(2).

[99] *See, e.g., Lawrence v. Florida,* 421 F.3d 1221 (11th Cir. 2005); *Miller v. Dragovich,* 311 F.3d 574 (3d Cir. 2002).

[100] *Abela v. Martin,* 348 F.3d 164, 170 (6th Cir. 2003).

[101] 127 S. Ct. at 1082.

[102] *Id.* at 1083 ("This Court is not a part of a 'state's post-conviction procedures.'").

[103] *Id.* ("The Courts of Appeals have uniformly interpreted 'direct review' in §2244(d)(1)(A) to encompass review of a state conviction by this Court. By contrast, §2244(d)(2) refers exclusively to '*state* post-conviction or other collateral review,' language not easily interpreted to include participation by a federal court.").

[104] *Id* at 1086.

[105] *Id.* at 1089.

[106] 127 S.Ct. 2842 (2007).

[107] *Panetti v. Quarterman,* No. 06-6407, Brief for Respondent On Writ of *Certiorari* To The United States Court Of Appeals For The Fifth Circuit, page i; Supplemental Brief for Respondent, page i.

[108] 127 S.Ct. at 2848.

[109] *Id.* at 2849.

[110] *Id.* at 2850-2851.

[111] *Id.* at 2851.

[112] 477 U.S. 399, 409-410 (1986)("The Eighth Amendment prohibits a State from carrying out a sentence of death upon a prisoner who is insane").

[113] *Panetti v. Dretke*, 401 F.Supp.2d 702, 705-706 (W.D. Tex. 2004).

[114] *Panetti v. Dretke*, 448 F.3d 815 (5th Cir. 2006).

[115] *Panetti v. Quarterman*, 127 S.Ct. 852 (2007).

[116] 127 S. Ct. at 2852.

[117] The Court will ordinarily decline to announce a "new rule," that is a first-time constitutional interpretation, in a habeas case, *Teague v. Lane*, 489 U.S. 288 (1989).

[118] *Id.* at 2853. 28 U.S.C. 2244(b)(2) states that, "A claim presented in a second or successive habeas corpus application under section 2254 that was not presented in a prior application shall be dismissed... ."

[119] *Id.* at 2854.

[120] Id.

[121] *Stewart v. Martinez-Villareal,* 523 U.S. 637 (1998)(In *Stewart*, the Court held that if an inmate brings a *Ford* claim in his first petition that is dismissed because it is not ripe, the inmate can bring the claim later when it becomes ripe; based on *Stewart* case, refiling the dismissed claim is basically just a continuation of the earlier claim dismissed on ripeness grounds).

[122] 127 S. Ct. at 2855. When considering a state inmate's habeas claim of a violation of federal law, Federal habeas courts must defer to state court decisions adjudicating the claim unless those decisions are "contrary to, or involve an unreasonable application of, clearly established" Supreme Court precedent, 28 U.S.C. 2254(d)(1).

[123] *Ford* was a 5-4 decision in which Justice Powell provided the fifth vote. Of the five, his was the most limited, and consequently controlling, statement on the question of how a State must proceed in the face of a claim that a death row inmate cannot be executed because of incompetence, which would include providing a hearing at which the prisoner has the opportunity "to submit 'evidence and argument from the prisoner's counsel, including expert psychiatric evidence that may differ from the state's own psychiatric examination.'"127 S.Ct. at 2585-2586, quoting Justice Powell's concurrence in *Ford*, 477 U.S. at 427.

[124] *Id.* at 2858.

[125] Id.

[126] Id.

[127] *Id.* at 2861. Although Panetti claimed "to understand 'that the state is saying that it wishes to execute him for his murders,' he believes in earnest that the stated reason is a 'sham' and the State in truth wants to execute him 'to stop him from preaching.'" *Id.* at 2860.

[128] *Id.* at 2862.

[129] *Id.* at 2864.

[130] Id.

[131] 127 S.Ct. 793, 797 (2007).

[132] 127 S. Ct. at 2866.

[133] *Id.* at 2866-2867.

In: Capital Punishment Update
Editor: Lorraine V. Coyne, pp. 99-114
ISBN: 978-1-60456-133-3

Chapter 4

CAPITAL PUNISHMENT: SUPREME COURT DECISIONS OF THE 2005-2006 TERM*

Paul Starett Wallace, Jr.

ABSTRACT

During the 2005-2006 Term, the Supreme Court gave favorable decisions to the defendants in three out of the six death penalty cases it announced. In *Hill v. McDonough,* the Court ruled unanimously that the method-of-lethal injection claims can be brought under 42 U.S.C. § 1983 rather than under the *habeas corpus* statute (28 U.S.C. §2254). In *House v. Bell*, a case involving a death row inmate who claimed that DNA evidence proved he did not commit the crime for which he was found guilty, the Court found in a 5 -3 ruling that the petitioner had satisfied the "gateway" standard for habeas review, but left open the question of whether the Constitution precludes execution of an "innocent" defendant found guilty and sentenced following a constitutionally adequate trial. In *Holmes v. South Carolina,* the Court unanimously held that a capital defendant cannot be denied the right to introduce evidence of third party guilt. The other cases, in which the Court upheld application of state death penalty statutes, appear to reveal a greater division among the justices over the fairness of capital punishment. The 5-4 decision in *Kansas v. Marsh* centered around a debate concerning capital punishment as much as it did a ruling on the unusual statute in Kansas which provided that juries should sentence a defendant to die – rather than serve life in prison – when the evidence for and against imposing death is equal. In

* Excerpted from CRS Report RL33621, dated August 23, 2006.

Brown v. Sanders, a second 5-4 decision, the Court upheld the petitioner's death sentence even though two of the sentencing factors presented to the jury were declared invalid. In *Oregon v. Guzek*, the Court held that states may reasonably refuse to allow convicted capital defendants to offer alibi evidence for the first time at the sentencing phase of their trials; two Justices would have permitted the exclusion of any evidence at sentencing that cast doubt upon the jury's guilty verdict, but the majority were obviously unwilling to go that far.

Introduction

The six capital punishment decisions which were decided during the 2005-2006 Term involved issues concerning: (1) a challenge to the lethal injection protocol as cruel and unusual punishment in violation of the 8th Amendment (*Hill v. McDonough)*, (2) constitutionality of a death penalty state statute that requires death if plus and minus factors are in balance (*Kansas v. Marsh*), (3) whether petitioner's compelling new evidence, though at the very least a colorable claim of actual innocence, was as a matter of law insufficient to excuse his failure to present that evidence before the state courts (*House v. Bell*), (4) disagreement among the courts regarding whether witness testimony was "mitigating evidence" (designed to spare the 18 year old from lethal injection) or "alibi evidence"(that went directly to whether the defendant was guilty) which should have been presented during the guilt or innocence phase of the trial (*Oregon v. Guzek*), (5) whether State's law governing admissibility of third-party guilt evidence violates the capital defendant's constitutional right to present a complete defense premised on due process, confrontation, and compulsory process clauses (*Holmes v. South Carolina*), and (6) whether a new trial is warranted if two of several aggravating factors found by the jury are later held to be invalid (*Brown v. Sanders*).

In three cases[1] the Court kept alive the appeals of the death row inmates in Florida, Tennessee, and South Carolina. In the other three cases[2], the Court affirmed the States' death penalty sentences.

Hill v. McDonough[3]

On June 12, 2006, the Court, held unanimously, that the use of lethal injection as a form of execution in the State of Florida constituted a challenge to the cruel and unusual provision of the Eighth Amendment and properly raised a claim under 42 U.S.C. § 1983, which provides a cause of action for civil rights violations, rather than under the *habeas corpus* provisions.

The petitioner (Hill) challenged Florida's injection protocol under 42 U.S.C. § 1983 as likely to cause him severe pain and suffering, but the lower courts construed his suit as a habeas petition under 28 U.S.C.§2254 and dismissed it as a procedurally barred second and successive petition.[4] In an opinion written by Justice Kennedy, the Court reversed noting the distinction between challenges to the lawfulness or duration of confinement, which must be brought via a *habeas corpus* petition, and challenges to the circumstances, which need not be.[5] The difference is that the former, but not the latter, necessarily challenges the legality of a sentence i.e., finding that a state cannot detain or execute an inmate in one particular manner does not mean that it cannot detain or execute him at all.[6] The reasoning of the Court in *Hill* was that although Florida law prescribed lethal injection as the means of execution, it left the specific method of injection up to the correction officials, and Hill challenged only the particular, three-drug sequence intended for his execution.[7] Inasmuch as Hill left open the possibility that Florida could execute him by lethal injection by another method, a decision in his favor under 42 U.S.C. § 1983 did not imply that his sentence by lethal injection generally is unlawful.[8]

The Court was sensitive to the concerns raised by Florida, the United States Solicitor General and others that death-row inmates will simply challenge individual aspects of their planned executions one at a time and thereby effectively block their executions.[9] Notwithstanding, the Court rejected a proposal to require prisoners such as Hill to identify in their complaints alternative means of execution that they would accept.[10] According to the Court, heightened pleading requirements should result from changes to the Federal Rules of Criminal Procedure similar to the specific pleading requirements which are mandated by the Federal Rules of Civil Procedure and not, as a general rule, by case-by-case litigation.[11] The Court also noted that filing a section 1983 action does not entitle an inmate to a stay of execution, which allows courts to consider factors such as whether a suit is speculative or filed too late in the day.[12] At least temporarily, the decision in *Hill* may delay executions as challenges to the constitutionality to the state's lethal injection method of execution are addressed and decided.

HOUSE V. BELL[13]

On June 12, 2006, the Court decided its second death penalty case in a 5-3 decision with Justice Kennedy joined by Justices Breyer, Stevens, Souter, and Ginsburg for the majority (Justice Alito did not participate). This case raised an issue which has hung over the imposition of capital punishment in recent years as it relates to newly discovered evidence and the possibility that an innocent person could be executed.

Paul House sought release from Tennessee's death row based on what his appeal to the Court calls "new reliable evidence" of innocence[14] which involves an application of the "miscarriage-of-justice" exception to the procedural default of state claims in federal court under *Schlup v. Delo*.[15] House claimed that DNA tests show that the semen found on the murder victim, Carolyn Muncey's clothes belonged to her husband, Hubert Muncey, and not to House, as a jury in Union County, Tenn., found 20 years ago. The lower federal courts rejected his claims.[16]

The issue before the Supreme Court was first how strong his case for innocence must be to qualify for habeas review in federal court.[17] In addition, House asked the Court to resolve an issue left open earlier and find the new evidence exonerated him.[18] Although the Court has not explicitly decided that it is unconstitutional to execute a convicted but innocent person, it suggested the possibility in 1993 in *Herrera v. Collins*.[19] There in a 5-4 opinion, however, it ruled that Leonel Torres Herrera had no right to reopen his case 10 years after his conviction, based solely on his claim of new proof of innocence.[20] Justices O'Connor and Kennedy joined that opinion without endorsing the suggestion and with the stipulation that they believed that there was little doubt of Herrera's guilt.[21]

The *House* Court referred to the standard of *Schup v. Delo* and held that it was more likely than not that no reasonable juror viewing the record as a whole would find House guilty beyond a reasonable doubt.[22] Justice Kennedy, writing for the majority, noted that "...'all the evidence, old and new, incriminating and exculpatory, without regard to whether it would necessarily be admitted under rules of admissibility that would govern at trial'" must be taken into account.[23] He stated that when an inmate comes to federal court with evidence of innocence, "[t]he court's function is not to make an independent factual determination about what likely occurred, but rather to assess the likely impact of the evidence on reasonable jurors."[24]

The majority decided that House's revelation about DNA and the blood stains were enough to overcome the strict standards that must be met before prisoners are allowed to re-argue issues of innocence long after their convictions.[25] They declined to reach, however, the question left open in *Herrera*, whether the Constitution precludes execution of an "actually innocent" defendant found guilty and sentenced in a constitutionally adequate trial.[26] Should such a right exist, House had failed present evidence of sufficient persuasion to claim it.[27]

Chief Justice Roberts, in the dissent, said the majority had ignored the trial judge's determination that House and several of his witnesses were unreliable. The Chief Justice also noted that the trial judge had found that Muncey's autopsy blood was spilled on House's jeans after the FBI already had determined that the blood on his pants belonged to the victim.[28] Justice Roberts' dissent agreed with the majority on the *Herrera* issue, but argued that despite the evidence, "the case against House remains substantially unaltered from the cases presented to the jury."[29] As a result, Justice Roberts said, the *Schlup* standard was not met.[30]

The judgment upholding the denial of *habeas corpus* relief was reversed, and the case was remanded for consideration of House's procedurally barred claims.

HOLMES V. SOUTH CAROLINA[31]

Holmes was convicted of multiple crimes, including first degree murder, and sentenced to death. At his trial, the court did not allow Holmes to present evidence that a third party had committed the crimes he had been charged with. On May 1, 2006, the Supreme Court, with Justice Alito writing the opinion for a unanimous Court, ruled that South Carolina had deprived Bobbie Lee Holmes of a fair trial when it prevented him from putting on evidence contradictory to the State's case and which also pointed to another possible suspect. The prosecution relied heavily on forensic evidence that strongly supported petitioner's guilt. The petitioner sought to rebut the State's forensic evidence by introducing expert testimony suggesting that the evidence had been contaminated and that the police had engaged in a plot to frame him. The petitioner also sought to introduce evidence that another man by the name of Jimmy McCaw White had been in the victim's neighborhood on the morning of the *assault* and White had either acknowledged petitioner's innocence or admitted to committing the crimes himself. In White's pretrial testimony, he denied making the incriminating statements and provided an alibi for the time of the assault.[32]

The trial court excluded petitioner's third-party guilt evidence citing the State Supreme Court's *Gregory* decision, which held that this evidence is admissible if it raises a reasonable inference as to the defendant's own innocence, but is inadmissible if it merely casts a bare suspicion or raises a conjectural inference as to another's guilt.[33] The State Supreme Court, affirming the trial court, cited both *Gregory* and its later decision in *Gay*,[34] and held that where there is strong forensic evidence of an appellant's guilt, gratuitous evidence regarding a third party's alleged guilt does not raise a reasonable inference as to the appellant's own innocence.[35] Applying this standard, the South Carolina State Supreme Court held that the petitioner could not overcome the forensic evidence against him.[36]

The U.S. Supreme Court granted *certiorari* based upon the question regarding whether South Carolina's rule governing the admissibility of third-party guilt evidence violates a criminal defendant's constitutional right to present a complete defense grounded in the Due Process, Confrontation, and Compulsory Process Clauses.[37]

The U.S. Supreme Court held that a criminal defendant's federal constitutional rights are violated by an evidence rule under which the defendant may not introduce evidence of third-party guilt if the prosecution has introduced forensic evidence that, if believed, strongly supports a guilty verdict.[38] The Court said:

> [S]tate and federal rulemakers have broad latitude under the Constitution to establish rules excluding evidence from criminal trials. This latitude, however, has limits. Whether rooted directly in the Due Process Clause of the Fourteenth Amendment or in the Compulsory Process or Confrontation clauses of the Sixth Amendment, the Constitution guarantees criminal defendants a meaningful opportunity to present a complete defense. This right is abridged by evidence rules that infringe] upon a weighty interest of the accused and are 'arbitrary' or 'disproportionate to the purposes they are designed to serve.'
>
> While the Constitution thus prohibits the exclusion of defense evidence under rules that serve no legitimate purpose or that are disproportionate to the ends that they are asserted to promote, well-established rules of evidence permit trial judges to exclude evidence if its probative value is outweighed by certain other factors such as unfair prejudice, confusion of the issues, or potential to mislead the jury. An application of this principle is found in rules regulating the admission of evidence proffered by criminal defendants to show that someone else committed the crime with which they are charged. Such rules are widely accepted and are not challenged here. In *Gregory*, the South Carolina Supreme Court adopted and applied a rule intended to be of this type. In *Gay* and this case, however, that court radically changed and extended the *Gregory* rule by holding that, where there is strong evidence of a defendant's guilt, especially strong forensic evidence, proffered evidence about a third party's alleged guilt may (or perhaps must) be excluded. Under this rule, the trial judge does not focus on the probative value or the potential

> adverse effects of admitting the defense evidence of third-party guilt. Instead, the critical inquiry concerns the strength of the prosecution's case: If the prosecution's case is strong enough, the evidence of third-party guilt is excluded even if that evidence, if viewed independently, would have great probative value and even if it would not pose an undue risk of harassment, prejudice, or confusion of the issues. Furthermore, as applied below, the rule seems to call for little, if any, examination of the credibility of the prosecution's witnesses or the reliability of its evidence.
>
> [The point of this is that] by evaluating the strength of only one party's evidence, no logical conclusion can be reached regarding the strength of contrary evidence offered by the other side to rebut or cast doubt. Because the rule applied below did not heed this point, the rule is `arbitrary' in the sense that it does not rationally serve the end that the *Gregory* rule and other similar third-party guilt rules were designed to further. Nor has the State identified any other legitimate end served by the rule. Thus, the rule violates a criminal defendant's right to have`a meaningful opportunity to present a complete defense.[39]

Justice Alito was guided by a string of Supreme Court decisions which were used as precedent to set up a balancing test to weigh and determine the opportunity for the defendant to present a complete defense.[40] In a situation where South Carolina's rule was that if the State had put on strong forensic evidence of the defendant's guilt, the defendant could be prohibited from raising an alternative theory of a third-party's guilt. Under these circumstances, the Court concluded that Holmes did not have a meaningful opportunity to present a complete defense. The Court decided that this rule was arbitrary and irrational for the reason "... that by evaluating the strength of only one party's evidence, no logical conclusion can be reached regarding the strength of contrary evidence offered by the other side to rebut or cast doubt."[41]

KANSAS V. MARSH[42]

On June 26, 2006, the Supreme Court narrowly upheld the death penalty in Kansas in a 5-4 decision which reversed the Kansas Supreme Court and ruled that the Kansas' death penalty statute does not violate the Eighth or Fourteenth Amendments when it allows imposition of the penalty should the jury determine that the aggravating and mitigating factors are of equal weight.

Marsh was convicted of capital murder, first-degree premeditated murder, and aggravated arson and burglary stemming from the deaths of Mary Anne Pasch and her 19-month-old daughter. The jury sentenced Marsh to death after finding the existence of three aggravating circumstances that were not outweighed by the mitigating circumstances. Marsh appealed his conviction, arguing that the trial court had erred in excluding, based on state law, his evidence connecting the woman's husband to the crime.[43]

During the time that Marsh's appeal was pending, the Kansas Supreme Court held in *State v. Lepas* that Kansas' death penalty statute – under which Marsh had been sentenced – was unconstitutional because it mandated a sentence of death when the aggravating and mitigating circumstances offset and counterbalanced each other.[44] The court held that the U.S. Supreme Court decision in *Walton v. Arizona,[45]* was not controlling because Arizona did not impose the death penalty when there was a tie between the aggravating and mitigating circumstances.[46] Notwithstanding, the Kansas Supreme Court attempted to salvage the death penalty in the *Claps* case by reconstructing the Kansas statute so that equipoise would not mandate the death penalty by construing it to mean that the aggravating circumstance(s) must "outweigh any mitigating circumstances found to exist" before capital punishment may be imposed.[47]

When Marsh appealed his death sentence in 2004, the Kansas Supreme Court held that its attempt to rewrite the language of the statute was in error because the process used to select which defendants are sentenced to death does not comport with the fundamental respect for humanity underlying the Eighth Amendment. The Kansas Supreme Court held that there was "no way" that Kansas' weighing equation is permissible under the Eighth and Fourteenth Amendments.[48]

Justice Thomas, writing for the 5-4 majority, said "our precedents establish that a state enjoys a range of discretion in imposing the death penalty...."[49] The decision reversed the Kansas Supreme Court decision which held that the law violated the Eighth Amendment's protection against cruel and unusual punishment. In upholding the Kansas statute, the U.S. Supreme Court cited *Walton v. Arizona*.[50] In *Walton*, the Court held that a state death penalty statute may give the defendant the burden to prove that mitigating circumstances outweigh aggravating circumstances.[51] Finding that *Walton* controlled , the Court reasoned that the Kansas' death penalty statute may constitutionally direct imposition of the death penalty when the State has proved beyond a reasonable doubt that mitigating circumstances do not outweigh aggravating circumstances, even when they are of equal weight.[52] Even if *Walton* did not directly control, the Court stated, a state has a range of discretion in imposing the death penalty, including how the aggravating and mitigating circumstances are weighed, as long as the state system satisfies the requirements of *Fermion v. Georgia* and *Gregg v. Georgia*.[53] The Court reasoned that the use of mitigation evidence is a product of the requirement of individualized sentencing.[54] The Court also found that the

Kansas death penalty statute rationally narrows the class of death-eligible defendants and allows a jury to consider any mitigating evidence that is relevant to its sentencing determination.[55]

Justice Souter, with Justices Stevens, Ginsberg, and Breyer joining, issued a dissenting opinion.[56] Justice Shouter noted that the Kansas statute would lead to death sentences in doubtful cases and "is obtuse by any moral or social measure."[57]

Justice Souter agrees with the Kansas Supreme Court that essentially, the Eighth Amendment forbids a mandatory death penalty in "doubtful cases", and that this is precisely what the Kansas statute does (that is, a case where mitigating factors equally balance aggravating factors is a "doubtful case" in Justice Shouters estimation)[58]. Justice Souter's concern is that in such a case, which he calls a tie, the tiebreaker has nothing to do with the details of the crime or any facts about the defendant, but that the statute presents mandatory death as the tiebreaker.[59] Justice Souter is troubled by this in light of the fact that the past decade has shown DNA test exonerating numerous death row defendants.[60] Citing the experience of Illinois, Justice Souter's dissent noted that 13 deathrow inmates were released between 1977 and 2000, triggering a state moratorium on executions, and referred to studies that he said, showed that dozens of death row inmates in other states were wrongly convicted.[61] Justice Scalia said the studies that Justice Souter cited are factually inaccurate, because many of the inmates they list as innocent were not exonerated but were released for technical legal reasons.[62]

OREGON V. GUZEK[63]

On February 22, 2006, the Supreme Court in an 8-0 decision (Justice Alito not participating), ruled that Oregon courts are not required to allow the defendant to introduce new alibi evidence pertaining to his innocence at the sentencing phase of the trial.[64] Two Justices, Scalia and Thomas, concurred in the result but would have recognized a state right to bar all residual doubt of guilty evidence from sentencing proceedings.[65]

Oregon tried Guzek, who was 18 at the time he was convicted, for the offense of capital murder. The evidence showed that Guzek and two associates decided to burglarize the Houser family home. After entering the home, an associate killed Rod Houser, and Guzek then robbed and killed Lois Houser. After the police learned that Guzek held a special grudge against the Housers, they traced and apprehended him and his associates. The associates confessed and testified at trial, painting Guzek as the ring leader.

Guzek's defense during the penalty phase of this trial rested in part upon an alibi. He presented two alibi witnesses, his grandfather and his mother, who testified that Guzek had been with one or the other at the time of the crime. The jury, disbelieving the alibi, sentenced him to death.

Guzek appealed and the Oregon Supreme Court affirmed the conviction; but the court ordered a new sentencing proceeding.[66] Guzek was again sentenced to death; he again appealed; and the Oregon Supreme Court again ordered re-sentencing.[67] Guzek was sentenced to death for the third time; he again appealed; and again the Oregon Supreme Court found the sentencing procedures faulty.[68] Seeking to avoid further errors at the next (the fourth) sentencing proceeding, the Oregon Supreme Court also addressed the admissibility of certain evidence Guzek sought to introduce at that proceeding, including live testimony from his mother concerning his alibi.[69]

The Oregon Supreme Court held that the Eighth and Fourteenth Amendments provide Guzek a federal constitutional right to introduce this evidence at his upcoming sentencing proceeding.[70] At the State's (Oregon) request, the U.S. Supreme Court agreed to review that issue under certiorari.[71]

During the sentencing phase of Guzek's trial, the defense tried to introduce witness testimony – "findings of fact" – that placed him away from the murder scene. The defense called this "mitigating evidence" designed to spare Guzek from lethal injection. Different courts have disagreed on whether it was actually "alibi evidence" that applied directly to whether a defendant was guilty and should have been presented during the guilt or innocence phase of the trial.[72]

The Supreme Court ruled that Oregon courts are not required to allow the defendant to introduce new alibi evidence pertaining to his innocence at the sentencing phase of the trial. The Court reasoned that states may put reasonable limits on the evidence a defendant may present.[73] Particularly at the sentencing phase, when the question is not whether the defendant committed the crime but how,[74] and since the issue of innocence had already been litigated, and the state law allows the defendant to present evidence of his innocence in the form of transcripts from his original trial by a jury, the Oregon court did not have to hear Guzek's additional evidence of innocence.[75]

Justices Scalia and Thomas concurred in the result but lamented that the Court had failed to take advantage of "the opportunity to put to rest, once and for all, the mistaken notion that the Eighth Amendment requires that a convicted capital defendant be given the opportunity, at his sentencing hearing, to present evidence and argument concerning residual doubts about his guilt."[76] Justice Alito took no part in the case.[77]

Brown v. Sanders[78]

On January 11, 2006, the Court in a 5-4 decision affirmed Sanders' death sentence and refined its death penalty jurisprudence by establishing a new rule: "an invalidated sentencing factor (whether an eligibility factor or not) will render the sentence unconstitutional by reason of its adding an improper element to the aggravation scale in the weighing process *unless* one of other sentencing factors enables the sentencer to give aggravating weight to the same facts and circumstances."[79]

Sanders was convicted of first-degree murder, attempted murder, robbery, burglary, and attempted robbery. The jury, at the guilt phase of his trial, found four "special circumstances" under California law, each of which independently rendered him eligible for the death penalty: (1) murder committed during the course of a robbery; (2) murder committed in the course of a burglary; (3) murder committed to prevent a witness from testifying; and (4) murder committed in an "especially heinous, atrocious, or cruel" manner.[80] At the penalty phase, the jury was instructed to consider a list of sentencing factors relating to the petitioner's background and the nature of the crime including "the circumstances of the crime to which the defendant was convicted in the present proceeding and the existence of any special circumstances found to be true."[81] The jury sentenced the defendant to death. The California Supreme Court, on direct appeal, set aside two of the four "special circumstances": the burglary-murder special circumstance under state merger law, and the "heinous, atrocious, or cruel" special circumstance because it had previously found this standard unconstitutionally vague.[82] However, it affirmed the death sentence, referring to the Supreme Court's decision in *Zant v. Stephens* to uphold a death sentence decision despite the invalidation of two of several aggravating factors.[83] The Supreme Court denied *cert* on direct appeal.[84]

Sanders then filed for federal *habeas*, which was denied at the district court level. The Ninth Circuit reversed, concluding that the California court had misapplied *Zant*, which is only applicable to non-weighing states, in upholding the verdict despite the invalidity of two of the special circumstances, because two others remained.[85] It determined California to be a weighing state, and applied the Court's decision in *Stringer v. Black* to mean that California courts could only uphold the death sentence by finding the jury's use of the invalidated special circumstances to be harmless beyond a reasonable doubt or by independently reweighing the factors.[86]

The Supreme Court reversed the Ninth Circuit's decision and held that no new trial was constitutionally required.[87] The Court established the rule that a jury's consideration and finding of an invalid sentencing factor taints any death verdict unless the same facts and circumstances evidence a valid sentencing factor also found by the jury.[88] The Court said that the existing valid aggravating factors which fit the description of the invalid factors were sufficient and therefore Sanders' death sentence was not "skewed" and neither did the invalid factors narrow the field "... of aggravating facts the jury was entitled to consider in determining sentence."[89]

Justice Scalia, joined by Chief Justice Roberts and Justice O'Connor, Kennedy, and Thomas, delivered the opinion of the Court. Justices Stevens and Souter dissented because they felt the majority's announcement of a new standard inappropriately complicated the law in the area.[90] Justices Breyer and Ginsberg dissented because they felt that in some situations impressing upon the jury that the facts and circumstances supported an invalid finding would taint the process even if the same facts and circumstances also supported and resulted in a valid finding.[91]

REFERENCES

[1] *Hill v. McDonough,* 126 S. Ct.2096 (2006); *House v. Bell,* 126 S.Ct. 2064 (2006); *Holmes v. South Carolina,* 126 S. Ct.1727 (2006).
[2] *Oregon v. Guzek,* 126 S. Ct. 1226 (2006); *Kansas v. Marsh,* 126 S. Ct. 2516 (2006); *Brown v. Sanders,* 126 S. Ct. 884 (2006).
[3] 126 S. Ct. 2096 (2006).
[4] *Hill v. Crosby,* 437 F.3d 1084, 1085 (11th Cir. 2006).
[5] 126 S. Ct. at 2101-2102.
[6] *Id.* at 2102.
[7] Id.
[8] Id.
[9] *Id.* at 2103.
[10] Id.
[11] Id.
[12] *Id.* at 2104.
[13] 126 S. Ct. 2064 (2006).
[14] *Id.* at 2077-2078.
[15] 513 U.S. 298 (1995) cited at 126 S. Ct. 2076-2077 (Justice Kennedy's majority opinion said that House's case fits under the rule announced in the 1995 case *Schlop v. Delo* which stated that innocence claims should reopen

appeals if, in light of new evidence, "it is more likely than not that no reasonable juror would have found the petitioner guilty").

[16] *House v. Bell*, 386 F.3d 668, 707-709 (6th Cir. 2004).

[17] 126 S.Ct. at 2087.

[18] *Id.* at 2086-87.

[19] 506 U.S. 390, 417 (1993)("We may assume, for the sake of argument in deciding this case, that in a capital case a truly persuasive demonstration of 'actual innocence' made after trial would render the execution of a defendant unconstitutional, and warrant federal habeas relief if there were no state avenue open to process such a claim. . . . .[T]he threshold showing for such an assumed right would necessarily be extraordinarily high. The showing made by petitioner in this case falls far short of any such threshold").

[20] *Id.* at 417-19.

[21] *Id.* at 419, 427 (O'Connor and Kennedy, JJ. concurring).

[22] 126 S.Ct. at 2076-2077.

[23] Id.

[24] *Id.* at 2077.

[25] *Id.* at 2087.

[26] *Id.* at 2086-87.

[27] *Id.* at 2087.

[28] *Id.* at 2092-2094.

[29] *Id.* at 2093.

[30] *Id.* at 2087. ("The question is not whether House was prejudiced at his trial because the jurors were not aware of the new evidence, but whether all the evidence, considered together, proves that House was actually innocent, so that no reasonable juror would vote to convict him.")

[31] 126 S. Ct. 1727 (2006).

[32] *Id.* at 1730-731.

[33] *State v. Gregory*, 198 S.C. 98, 104, 16 S.E.2d 532, 534 (1941).

[34] *State v. Gay*, 343 S.C. 543, 541 S.E.2d 541 (2001).

[35] *State v. Holmes*, 361 S.C. 333, 342-43, 605 S.E.2d 19, 24 (2004).

[36] Id.

[37] Holmes v. South Carolina, 126 S.Ct.34 (2005).

[38] 126 S.Ct. at 1728.

[39] *Id.* at 1728-1729 (internal citations omitted).

[40] *I.e., United States v. Schaefer*, 523 U.S. 303 (1998); *Rock v. Arkansas*, 483 U.S. 44 (1987); *Crane v. Kentucky*, 476 U.S. 683 (1986); *Chambers v. Mississippi*, 410 U.S. 284 (1973); *Washington v. Texas*, 388 U.S. 14 (1967).

[41] *Id.* at 1735.

[42] 126 S. Ct. 2516 (2006).

[43] *Id.* at 2520-521.

[44] *State v. Claps*, 272 An. 894, 899-903, 40 P.3d 139, 166-67 (2001). The Kansas statute (An. Stat. Ann. §21-4624(e)) provided that juries should sentence a defendant to die – rather than serve life in prison – when the evidence for and against imposing death were equal.

[45] 497 U.S. 639, 649-51 (1990), overruled on other grounds, *Ring v. Arizona*, 536 U.S. 584 (2002)(upholding Arizona's death penalty statute that burdened the defendant with establishing mitigating evidence sufficient to justify leniency once the state has established an aggravating factor).

[46] 272 An. at 1006-1007, 40 P.3d at 226.

[47] 272 An. at 1018, 40 P.3d at 234.

[48] 278 An. at 534-45, 102 P.3d at 457-64.

[49] 126 S. Ct. at 2525.

[50] *Id.* at 2522, citing *Walton v. Arizona* 497 US 639 at 645.

[51] *Id.* at 2523.

[52] *Id.* at 2524.

[53] *Id.* at 2519, citing, *Fermion v. Georgia*, 408 U.S. 238 (1972) and *Gregg v. Georgia*, 428 U.S. 153 (1976).

[54] *Id.* at 2523.

[55] *Id.* at 2526.

[56] *Id.* at 2541 (Souter, Stevens, Ginsberg and Breyer, JJ. dissenting).

[57] *Id.* at 2546.

[58] Id. at 2543.

[59] *Id.* at 2542

[60] Id at 2544.

[61] *Id* at 2544- 2545.

[62] *Id* at 2531- 2535.

[63] 126 S. Ct. 1226 (2006).

[64] *Id.* at 1230-231.

[65] *Id.* at 1233-234 (Scalia and Thomas, JJ. dissenting).

[66] *State v. Guzek*, 310 Ore. 299, 307, 797 P.2d 1031, 1036 (1990).

[67] *State v. Guzek*, 322 Ore. 245, 271, 906 P.2d 272, 287 (1995).

[68] *State v. Guzek*, 336 Ore. 424, 464, 86 P.3d 1106, 1129 (2004).

[69] 336 Ore. at 456-63, 86 P.3d at 1124-128.

[70] Id.

[71] *Oregon v. Guzek*, 544 U.S. 998 (2005).

[72] Justice Scalia's concurrence lists a series of state and lower federal court cases that had held that a capital defendant had no right to offer at sentencing mitigation evidence of residual doubt as to his guilt, 126 S.Ct. at 1234 (Scalia and Thomas, JJ. dissenting), citing, *Zeigler v. Crosby,* 345 F.3d 1300, 1310 (11th Cir. 2003); *Evans v. Thompson,* 881 F.2d 117, 121 (4th Cir. 1989); *Duest v. State,* 855 So.2d 33, 40-41 (Fla.2003); *Commonwealth v. Fisher,* 572 Pa. 105, 115-116, 813 A.2d 761, 767 (2002); *People v. Emerson,* 189 Ill.2d 436, 501-504, 245 Ill.Dec. 49, 727 N.E.2d 302, 338-339 (2000); *State v. Fletcher,* 354 N.C. 455, 470-472, 555 S.E.2d 534, 544 (2001); *Melson v. State,* 775 So.2d 857, 898-899 (Ala.Crim.App.1999).

[73] 126 S.Ct.at 1232.

[74] Id.

[75] *Id.* at 1233.

[76] *Id.* at 1233 (Scalia and Thomas, JJ. concurring in the judgment).

[77] *Id.* at 1233.

[78] 126 S. Ct. 884 (2006).

[79] *Id.* at 892 (emphasis in the original).

[80] *Id.* at 893.

[81] *Id.* at 888.

[82] *People v. Sanders*, 51 Cal.3d 471, 515-20, 273 Cal.Rptr. 537, 563-65, 797 P.3d 561, 587-99 (1990).

[83] 51 Cal.3d at 520-21, 273 Cal.Rptr. at 565-66, 797 P.3d at 589-90.

[84] *Sanders v. California*, 500 U.S. 948 (1991).

[85] *Sanders v. Woodford*, 373 F.3d 1054, 1062-67 (9th Cir. 2004).

[86] Id.

[87] 126 S.Ct. at 894.

[88] Or to repeat the words of the Court, "[a]n invalidated sentencing factor (whether an eligibility factor or not) will render the sentence unconstitutional by reason of its adding an improper element to the aggravation scale in the weighing process unless one of the other sentencing factors enables the sentencer to give aggravating weight to the same facts and circumstances." *Id.* at 892.

[89] 126 S. Ct. at 892-893.

[90] *Id.* at 895-96 (Stevens and Shouter, JJ. dissenting).

[91] *Id.* at 903 (Brewer and Ginsberg, JJ. dissenting)("the problem before us is not a problem of admissibility of evidence. It is a problem of the emphasis given that evidence by the State or the trial court. If that improper emphasis

is strong enough, it can wrongly place a thumb on death's side of the scale").

Index

D

E

F

G

M

N

O

P

Q

R

S

T

U

V

W